SELF ESTEEM

Confidence Building

Overcome Fear, Stress and Anxiety

Self Help Guide

3rd edition

by James Seals

Table of Contents

Introduction

Do you ever feel like that panic button is about to go off? We all do from time to time, but recognizing it and doing something about it are two different things. When you feel insecure, it is hardly likely to boost your confidence and self-esteem. Anxiety, once it is understood, is actually quite easy to come to terms with, but the first step in this long journey begins when you admit that you need help and decide to come looking for it. This book may just have been written with you in mind. The fact that you have come as far as reading this introduction says that you are looking for solutions. Often these can be found all on your own and you can move forward into a stage of your life when you understand yourself better and are able to drop all of your self-esteem issues.

Fear and anxiety are just a small part of the full picture and the exercises given in this book will help you to get beyond it so that you can find your own equilibrium and move forward in a much more positive manner. Many of the complexes that people have are as a result of the interactions that they have had within their lives. Those interactions or bad experiences leave their mark and it is only when you step beyond the fear that you actually get to realize your dreams and begin to live life to the fullest.

Are you afraid of life? We all are at some stage or other, but this book addresses that too because there is a recognized way to get beyond it and to learn how to trust life again. Until you do, you will not find a permanent state of happiness because you are too grounded in what you know and that holds you back. Take a journey through this book with us and decide before opening the first page that your life is worth exploring and that it is worth helping yourself to make your future life happy, fearless and filled with good things.

Others have taken this path and have found their lives enriched because their lack of understanding was what was holding them back. When you understand how self-esteem works and what you can do to correct it, you are able to move forward with confidence putting all of those bad experiences behind you and being able to look the world squarely in the face. Then you will know that your self-esteem issues are a thing of the past. This book provides exercises that you can use to develop and hone your self-perception skills to make you see yourself in a different light. It teaches you how to cope with criticism. It shows you why another person's opinion may not be as valuable as you think it is. In the exercises throughout the book, you will learn to hone in on the instincts that your mind is made up from and use these to help guide you toward the future.

The book also teaches you how to trust people and most of all how to learn to trust yourself. The trust is always going to be lacking when self-esteem issues exist. You are shown the different scales of self-esteem, and how high self-esteem can be every bit as negative as low self-esteem, so that you can watch your progress and mark your own chart as you feel that you are getting more confidence in yourself.

As you do the exercises, remember the reason that they were written. They were written to help you to get out of this phase of your life where everything seems negative and out of your control and to help you to see things in perspective. Your response to panic events is also touched upon so that you can see the benefit of slowing down sufficiently to think things through, while learning breathing techniques to make your panic response into a much more confident type of response.

Are you afraid of meeting people? The book has you covered from this perspective because you need all of that information that enriches your life and makes it a better place for you to be. You only have one life and the better job you do at using it to attain happiness, the less life you waste away.

Walk through the pages, but remember to backtrack when you need to. If you have an area of particular weakness, do the exercises over and over until they are successful for you and provide you with all that you need to move forward in a positive manner. Fears, perceptions, intuition, relating to others and every issue you can think of is covered within the pages of this book.

You should keep this as your guide to life until you have managed to get beyond feeling like you are not good enough or that you do not measure up. Everyone has the same capacity to measure up and the book guides you in a direction that is not only logical but is based on real life experience. How do I know it works? The book is an accumulation of my experiences put together, so that you don't have to rely upon trial and error in your life. I have done the homework for you. Now all you have to do is read the book and find out how to apply each of the exercises within its pages to your own life. Once you do, life becomes richer and you will be thrilled with the results.

You will also be shown how to create acceptable boundaries which will help you to deal with self-esteem issues, so that these do not come back to haunt you in the future. Once you have set boundaries, you know where the line is drawn and are able to move forward knowing that the ground upon which you are stepping with new relationships is sound. There is so much waiting out in the world for you to enjoy. Fear, stress and anxiety can block your pathway to actually finding that peace of mind that everyone seeks. This book has you covered from that point of view as well, because the more you learn about how to put your fear, stress and anxiety aside, the more space you have in your life for good things.

The mind, body and spirit need nourishment sometimes and you will learn why because this is very relevant to the way that you relate to others and the way that you face your life ambitions. They are all out there ready for you to grab the opportunities and make the most of them. The problem is that at this juncture, you are unsure of your footing. We will put that right. Imagine someone standing in the middle of a river on a rocky stone. When you have anxiety issues, that's you. Choose the wrong way forward and you fall in. However, now imagine a plant that has deep roots and can protect itself against the winds and tempests. That's how you need to be in order to overcome all of the hurdles that life has a habit of putting in the way.

Chapter 1 – What Thoughts Are All About

There are several kinds of thoughts that you can have. You already know that, of course, but did you know how the thoughts that you keep thinking impact your life? If they are negative and fearful, you can expect negativity and fearfulness to follow. Your mind believes that you have something to fear and by repeating these thoughts, what you do is reinforce it as fact, when in fact, it is not.

Let's look at a progression of how ideas and thoughts gain power to really control the way that we see ourselves and the world around us. At first in the very vague and esoteric sense, we have what comes to us as ideas. Ideas originate from the imagination, and while this area of thinking can be influenced by external stimuli, sometimes we find ourselves having ideas of no particular origin.

Being so slippery and intangible, ideas will come and go throughout our day and in our sleep in dreams. Usually we are not very aware of all this activity until – oh! There's one! – We come across an idea that captures our interest and we hang on to it, and sometimes we will write it down or record it in some other way. This all begins as entertainment without being taken too seriously, and so we can understand that ideas are neutral and can easily be changed.

When we begin to ruminate on a vague idea, we are engaging in the thought process, so all interpretations that come from this one idea can be considered thoughts, and the number of thoughts for this process can go on endlessly. They can repeat themselves, they can take on different forms and still imply the same thing, and they can lead to a mess of other thoughts via tangents that might end up being completely irrelevant to the original idea. Once we develop a number of thoughts that reinforce, support and expand that original idea, what we have now is a belief. Because beliefs are considered to have so many other thoughts to back them up, they give off the illusion of being legitimate, and so they are more difficult to change.

Beliefs can aid in supporting a particular way of life, and they do have the tendency to change as the world changes, however when we construct beliefs around other groups of beliefs and convince ourselves that all of them are true and valid, we have created a religion. Religion does not have to be about a concept of God. Anything that is practiced as a way of life that guides and determines what course of action we take in living that life can be considered a religion. Science is a religion. And yes, low self-esteem and even high self-esteem in the form of an overdeveloped sense of pride can be religions.

This is how ideas and thoughts turned into beliefs become so powerful, and also potentially dangerous. Because beliefs are so complex and can be interpreted in a number of ways, people often commit heinous actions in the name of a belief that are actually contrary to the core message of that particular belief, but they find ways to place emphasis on one particular thought of that belief system to justify their actions. We will dive deeper into this later in the chapter about love and self-love. For now, let's get back to the nature of thoughts.

Thoughts decide upon the course of your life and they are added to by interactions with other people and the way that people reflect back on us. We cannot control that side of things, but we can control what happens in our own minds. For example, let's show you how a child is influenced by a parent and then goes on to thinking in a fearful or negative way:

- Child: I can't tie my shoe laces

- Parent: Why are you so useless?

- Child: I forgot to bring my homework books home

- Parent: You really are stupid

What you can see from this is that the child is made to believe in their own stupidity and uselessness. The child may fear actually telling the parent that they cannot do something or that they have forgotten something, so fear comes into the picture as well. Every time the child expressed being unable to do something, the thoughtless parent reminds the child of how stupid he or she is. This reinforces what the child begins to believe of him or herself.

Thoughts determine our reality. Negative and self-depreciating thoughts will impair us in ways we could not even fathom because their effect is so subtle and often they are ingrained in us from other people's and society's views at a very early age. When we are so young, from the ages of one to three, we absorb every single stimulus in our environment so vividly and we are so impressionable that they begin to take shape in our subconscious and form a basis for our own personal beliefs without our even realizing it. This is how incriminating beliefs perpetuate, because they are taught to us either actively or passively from the generations before us and get passed down throughout the ages.

At such young ages, we are very prone to the influence of our emotional reactions, however they are temporary. If you ever take a look at the nature of a child, you will find that their varying emotional states are fluid and temporary. If you go to a playground and witness children playing together, you might find that one child falls down and hurts themselves or another gets upset because a child has taken their toy away from them. But do they stay this way throughout the remainder of the day? No, they do not. In other words, do they allow their emotional state to take control of their actions and prevent them from enjoying themselves for a dragged out period of time? You will see that actually, the child will be upset for a few moments, but then they go right back to playing again or find something else to engage in that captivates their attention in a positive way. Their sustained behavior always comes back to happiness. So why is that?

Children are very in tune with their environment because they are open and captivated by all the different things that they interact with. They do not fall prey to the ongoing slew of analytical thinking that plays out scenarios that have not even happened. They also do not get caught up in speculation on what is or is not, what should or should not be, or what could or could not be. They are simply in a state of perpetual newness, which allows them to take each situation that comes to them in the moment at that particular moment, and when it is through, they move on to the next one without getting stuck in the past. That way, everything remains new to them and they are able to see every activity with a fresh perspective, which promotes a sense of wonder and enjoyment for taking life as it comes.

This kind of mentality leaves them open and vulnerable that some could consider being a double-edged sword, but it is only in this state that they are allowed to learn so much, being the adaptable little sponges that they are. For most children, they are not concerned with protecting themselves from the elements, which leaves them available for new opportunities to arise at every moment and take advantage of their creativity, as well as creating opportunities themselves with little effort. Despite the consequences of growing up and whatever we may convince ourselves of being the reality of the world (which oftentimes is another's point of view anyways, thus we have been convinced by someone else), we all began our lives with a very palpable and healthy level of self-esteem at some point. Having come this far and endured so much from living in this world, we have simply forgotten what we are capable of. This book, along with all other resources of positive reinforcement such as your good friends, encouraging family members and authorities of healthy living in body, mind, and spirit are all with you to help you remember your true self as a confident, capable, and worthwhile person.

Having shared that, we can see that the flexibility of a child's natural state gives them much room to grow and expound upon their curiosity without having to process the why's and what if's that states of low self-esteem put us through, as well as preventing ourselves from going after what we really might enjoy because of fears of embarrassment, incapability, and past events that we have convinced ourselves were a bad experience. These past experiences may well have felt bad in the moment, but that is because we were unaware of how to handle ourselves at that time. The truth is that every experience, whether good or bad, really serves as an excellent learning opportunity to navigate through life with our unique character. The better that we know ourselves and what we are willing to accept as true about ourselves, the better we become at navigating life for our own benefit and the benefit of others.

At young ages, because we are so impressionable, it is rare for children to know themselves so well that they refuse to take on negative criticisms from others. This especially goes for our parents, who we are naturally inclined to trust and look up to since they take care of us and serve as our protectors. What we fail to realize at these susceptible ages is that our parents are people too – they are human, they are imperfect, they have their own doubts, fears, issues, misconceptions about the world, and they make mistakes just like anybody else. But through the innocence of a child's eyes, we naively see them as perfect people. So when our imperfect parents project their own issues and ill-conceived views upon us, we take them to heart, believing that they are true. Then we become trained to see ourselves in a similar way as well as the world around us like this, and the cycle of self-depreciation and low self-esteem continues until we teach ourselves to know better.

You can never control other people's views of who you are, but you can control what you think of yourself as you get older. However, old habits die hard. You need to face the fact that as long as you believe yourself to be inadequate, you will be. Your beliefs and your thoughts dictate who you are or who other people see as being you. Thus, if you can change the pattern of those thoughts, you can improve who you are. You must be the one to take the initiative and claim yourself back. Others can positively reinforce your image for you with compliments and praise, but because of the way our tricky little minds work, no other person's opinions will be as powerful on us as the ones that we claim for ourselves.

When we take on other people's negative views and they affect our self-esteem, it is because we have allowed ourselves to believe what the other person was saying to be true. We take those views on as our own, and with a person who already has low self-esteem, another's negative views act as reinforcement to the falsities we have allowed ourselves to believe. In the same way, with low self-esteem it may be nice to hear another compliment us on a particular trait of ours, like how well someone paints for example, but unless we allow ourselves to actually believe it, that positivity just slides off of us instead of sinking in. We actually do the job for those past negative reinforcing people by criticizing ourselves even when we receive praise and find ourselves saying, "Oh thank you, that is a nice thing to say but no, it is not really good at all."

Stop beating yourself up for having made mistakes. It really does not matter and everyone does it. However, those who dwell on their mistakes find they haven't got room to see all the positive attributes that they have.

Exercise at controlling thought

Thoughts are controllable. From one moment to the next, you have the power to control what goes through your mind. You can switch things off or start to think of other things and this is where real control comes into the picture. The problem is that your mind is too filled with thoughts, so how do you distinguish between those that are immediately important and those that are totally unnecessary?

When thoughts are flowing so rapidly through your mind that they literally keep you up at night, it is called 'mind racing.' Mind racing is often related to those types of frivolous thoughts that may seem so important at the time because they revolve around an issue that we are convinced is actually important, as it may well be, although the volume of thinking that you commit to it is unnecessary.

For example say you were planning to meet up with a friend, you had spoken to them in advance as to where you would meet and what you would be doing and you both agreed to it. The time comes, and although you were ten minutes late because you got caught up letting the dog out before you left, you arrive to the designated place in time, such as a café. Yet your friend is not there. So you wait. You wait a long time, and with each new person passing into the café you anticipate the arrival of your friend, but they are not coming. You try to call and send messages to them over the phone but you do not receive any reply. The slow feeling of anxiety starts to build up and thoughts begin to race through your head, trying to figure out what has happened.

You think to yourself, "Did they get fed up with waiting for me even though I was a few minutes late?" "Are they put off about something I did in the past?" "Did something happen to them while they were on their way here?" "Did they get into an accident?" "Are they ok?" This type of thinking goes on for a while and you take it home with you when you finally decide to leave the café. The meeting and your friend are important to you, and you feel hurt that you had been stood up. If you have low self-esteem, this situation exacerbates it and your thoughts may regress into self-depreciation and victimization: "What is wrong with me?" "Why can't I do anything right?" Or maybe in your distress your sadness turns into anger: "Well if that is how they are going to be about it then I just won't bother with them anymore!" or "The next time I talk to them I am going to give them a piece of my mind!" But you will not be giving them the peace of your mind, because you have worked yourself up in so much uncontrolled speculation when the truth is you do not really have any idea what had happened. You could spend half the night wondering what happened and feeding into your emotional hurt, fueled by your low self-esteem.

The next morning you wake up feeling groggy and go to work with a cloudy mind, feeling irritable, and performing worse than usual. A few of your less sensitive coworkers notice and give you a hard time for it, adding to your frustration and now you are officially having a bad day. A few days pass and you may still be feeling poorly but are less clear as to why. A week later, you hear from your friend and all you remember is being angry with them. You answer, "What do you want?" and your friend replies, "Are you ok? What is wrong?" So you tell them that they ditched you last week. So then your friend apologizes and explains that their phone had died and while they were getting ready to go out, their brother from out of town came in for a surprise visit and they completely forgot about meeting up with you.

While the friend made a mistake, they cannot be blamed for your emotions because we are all responsible for our own emotions. No one can make us feel any particular way. We choose the way we feel, whether we are aware of it or not, and we must learn to take control over the thoughts that feed into those emotions by reinforcing them with positive thoughts. We must convince ourselves to think positively in order to move beyond habitual states of negative emotion and negative thinking to regain a healthy state of mind and sense of wellbeing. We will talk about active ways to help change our thought processes for the better later in the chapter on meditation.

Thoughts about yesterday or the past

These are thoughts that serve no purpose. You may have seen them as a protection mechanism against making the same mistakes, but they actually do not serve you very well at all. You cannot do anything about what is in the past, so you need to clear these thoughts out of your mind as much as possible. Drop the past because it is gone and you cannot live it again. You cannot change anything you did. You can only move on because life gives you no choice. If you are forever living in the past, you do not actually give yourself time for the present and that is bad news. The moments of your life are ticking away in a very unfruitful manner. You do not have confidence because you expect your mind to stagnate in past events. That is hardly fair, is it?

Thoughts and worries about the future

The future does need a certain amount of planning and you would be wrong to think otherwise. However, worrying about it will not change it. Yes, you can plan on what you will wear tomorrow or who you will see. You can look forward and anticipate, and that is a good thing because it gets you excited about life, but if you bring dread into the picture you are wasting an opportunity. Tomorrow has not happened yet. Your worries and concerns cannot change what does happen.

Thinking about and trying to plan for the future works to a certain extent as far as what you will do in the day and how prepared you will be for that next business presentation, but there are also so many undeterminable factors that you cannot plan for. Filled up parking lots, traffic jams, flight delays, absenteeism, brain farts, and your coworker's new and distracting hairstyle are always going to happen sooner or later, so you are much better off staying loose and present. That way worrying about future events will hardly be an issue because you will understand that life can lose its marbles but you do not have to when you accidentally find one by tripping on it – you can be centered in yourself to just roll with it instead.

It is so important to realize that you can only control your life to a certain extent. All of the events in the world, even down to the smallest unexpected things, will constantly be throwing you curveballs and you cannot stop it from happening. You have to learn to roll with the punches. You have to become flexible. Once you start directing your thoughts to working on this and letting go of worrying about control and making things perfect, your life will become much easier and you will find yourself laughing a lot more too.

Try to think only positive thoughts about tomorrow, if you must indeed think about it at all. Anything other than that is a waste of space in your mind. Any worries will actually take away positivity from this moment in time. The moments you spend worrying are totally wasted.

Thoughts about this moment

The latest way of thinking is that being aware of every moment makes it a much nicer place to be in, but it is not as simple as that. Psychologists are very aware of the new movement toward mindfulness and have seen the benefits of this because what it does is make you live in the NOW. Actually with more research and worldly exploration, you will find that the concepts of living in the moment and consistent mindfulness and awareness are not new at all. In fact, they are thousands of years old. They only appear new to us here in the western world because they are gaining popularity on mainstream levels. As the demands of urban and globalized living increase to levels that many people are not prepared to keep up with, mental adjustment and expansion become much needed. They are necessary to avoid the stress and sleep deprivation that this speedy and hectic pace of living involves.

We are kept so busy trying to make a living, sustain a comfortable lifestyle, organize and attend events and just find a moment's rest that we are almost deprived of our natural and necessary practice to process all of this information. This also goes along with processing our emotions so that we may have a clear view and understanding of where we are actually going in life and what the implications of our actions really take to effect. It becomes a part of waking up to reality – the real reality of life as we make it happen – and taking an active role in choosing what we really want our lives to look like.

The past is gone – the future is not here yet – and mindfulness insists that you concentrate on what is happening now. So how do you go about thinking only of now? It takes practice but you can do it and we will teach you how, so that the information that you gain is of use to you in your life. So you can put all your worries behind you and start living to your fullest capacity.

Making a safe place for your mind to be

Since you have not yet been introduced to mindfulness, let's try something easy for you for your first exercise. Close your eyes in a place where you will not get disturbed and think about something within your life where you felt happy and content. It may be an event that you are proud of, a sunny afternoon as a child or a place that you associate happy thoughts with. Visualize this positive thing – whatever it is – and feel the happiness flow over you. Feel the smile grow over your face and your muscles relax. Good things that we are proud of or that made us feel warm inside are always good things to use to help us overcome fears. They can also be used to focus the mind when things are negative.

Now go on through your day, but the first time that you feel fearful, step back into that comfortable place that you chose as your haven. You do not even need to close your eyes this time. You can be anywhere you want to be. As soon as a negative thought hits your mind, replace it with thoughts of that place that is your haven.

If you practice this for a while, you will find that you are in control of your thoughts. At this stage, it is not expected that you will not have any negative thoughts. It is only a starting point. However, you will learn how to put these out of your mind entirely by the end of the book. For now, be content that you have found a place you can go to when things seem negative. Keep a diary of your progress if you like, as this gives you a reference to refer to later to see how much progress you have made.

When you put yourself in control of your thoughts, you do something else as well. You divert your mind away from all the bad things that you might otherwise think about and that is a good practice to get into. Which kind of friend would you rather have?

- Someone who is perpetually unsure of himself?
- Someone who only has negative things to say?
- Someone who seems happy?

The point is that people who are happy attract more friends and with those friendships comes a support system to assist in sustaining that happiness. By replacing negative thoughts with positive imagery and taking your mind to that favorite place of comfort, you begin to get out of the funk of always thinking in a negative manner. You are not much use as a friend if you cannot remove yourself from negativity. Smile at the world and see how your life changes.

Similarly use this exercise in everyday life. Instead of thinking in a negative way, look around you at positive things. Is the sun shining, are the flowers coming out, what's that wonderful aroma? Mindfulness is all about recognizing the cup as half full instead of half empty and seeing all the good in life rather than concentrating on the negative aspects of life.

Chapter 2 – Observing Others

Many people learn from observation while others who have fears and negativity go through their lives without noticing anything, so they cannot learn what makes people confident and happy. What makes some succeed where others fail? If you take the time to observe, much of what makes the difference is common sense approach.

Exercise in observation

To find out more about other people, you need to take yourself to a place where people go and observe them. A crowded station or an airport lounge, a local mall or even the local market can all be places where you can observe people. This can be a fun and enriching experience, and it will help you to gain a lot of insight about recognizing the subtleties that people express in their body language and overall demeanor.

Recognizing confidence

Confidence is something that most people can recognize, but why? What is it that confident people display that people like you have trouble with? Let's try and show you. There is a girl on the corner over there that looks confident. She is well dressed, she smiles a lot and she seems happy and content. She looks really pretty but when you look closely, she is not that pretty. The look you get from her of initially being very pretty is because of her confidence. People who ooze confident can be quite plain, but they have learned how to exude confidence all the same. Look at her body language. She does not slouch. She holds her head up high and she is not scared to meet others by looking them in the eye. Anyone who practices that can do the same.

There are several ways to recognize and portray confidence and the lack thereof, many of which begin with body language. These signs are so prevalent, we often do them without being aware of them and they have been proven to be reflected at a very primal level throughout nature too. Primates, birds and even insects exert these expressions of confidence and insecurity the same as humans, so let's take a look at the varying representations to see what they imply and how they affect us.

From a very basic viewpoint, the difference between confident body language and insecure body language is the same as being open versus being closed. It makes sense because when we are open, we welcome chance and opportunity and we are ready for anything. When we are closed, it is an instinct to protect ourselves from these same elements because we have been hurt before, we are unsure of ourselves, and/or we are unsure of how to handle a situation. Insecure body language is displayed with arms crossed in front of the body, crossed legs, slouching, a hunched back and shoulders, head looking down and so on. When someone is holding their neck or has their hand up near their collarbone this has been shown to be a sign of extreme insecurity. Tense muscles and constant shifting are also characteristic of insecure body language. Avoiding eye contact is sometimes considered to be rude by others, but the truth is that perhaps that person is just not comfortable with themselves or being around other certain people and so they cannot bring themselves to look other people in the eyes when they are talking to them.

People who readily feel anxiety or stress usually have high amounts of cortisol in their bodies. Cortisol is a stress hormone that is primarily associated with the 'fight or flight' response. It serves us well in times of immediate danger when we feel our life is threatened. However, being under constant stress, whether it is self-induced because of an overdeveloped sense of insecurity or because we are constantly enduring stressful events in our lives, will keep our cortisol levels high. So having excess amounts of this when your life is not in danger can wreak havoc on your body, your mind, and your overall sense of wellbeing. On top of that, it has been shown that maintaining these postures that show insecurity also sustain raised levels of cortisol.

We can categorize confident body language into that which is relaxed and open. This means your head stands out tall and comfortably from your shoulders that are dropped, your chest sticks out a bit, and your stance is erect. Poses like putting your hands at your hips with your elbows out or standing over a table with your hands resting on top of it and out wide are all exertions of confidence. If you have ever seen the victory pose for sports players, they have their arms wide up over their head and their head tilted back a bit in celebration. Studies have shown that even athletes who are blind, that have never seen this pose, make the same gestures in a victory. This tells us that these expressions are innate and universal. When sitting down, slightly spread legs and the arms held out with hands clasped back behind the head is another expression of confidence. It says, "This is me, you get what you see."

Interestingly enough, these studies have also taken physiology, or the chemical levels in our body primarily dealing with hormones, into account. They looked at levels of testosterone, a confidence booster, in both men and women before and after having them practice these confidence poses for just a few minutes. The results were incredible. They showed that just by practicing simple postures such as those described earlier, there was a boost in these people's testosterone levels, meaning that not only does the mind affect the body as we have been talking about, but the body can affect the mind as well. These poses also reduced levels of cortisol, the stress hormone. So I encourage you to practice these poses on your own at home for minutes at a time and notice the difference. When you feel bold enough, casually practice them out in public as well.

At home exercise 1

Use a full-length mirror. Take a real hard look at yourself walk into a room. Look at your body language. People who are scared of life tend to approach everything in a timid manner and they usually get out of life what they expect because of this. Now, hold your head high, wear shoes that you can walk in without tripping over and keep your shoulders back. Take the frown off your face and look at how much more attractive you are when you walk into a room in this way, rather than your usual way. It makes a world of difference in the way that people perceive you and your interaction with others will alter in a very positive manner.

At home exercise 2

You will need a mirror for this exercise as well, although it can be any size as long as you can see your full face. Look at yourself in the mirror and look straight into your eyes. Take note of how just doing this makes you feel. Then, while looking into your eyes, say that you love yourself. Say, "I love you," as if you were speaking to another person that you really care for and be sincere about it. Except this is you, so you should say it and mean it. This can be difficult for some people, but that is ok. These people have just not spent enough time giving themselves the credit and attention that they deserve. After you say, "I love you," be your own friend and your own personal coach. Talk to you in a manner that you are giving quality attention to yourself. Tell yourself why you love you – list all the positive attributes that you like about yourself – these things can be physical, but you can dig deeper. Go as deep as you can. Keep it positive. Ensure that you are here for you, and thank yourself for working at it. Thank yourself for giving you the attention you deserve.

Recognizing Self-Confidence Problems

When you are observing people, look out for the signs that someone has self-confidence problems. These are people who need to overcompensate in public for their perceived inadequacies. They may speak out of turn in conversations and be too imposing. They may not recognize how to behave with friends and be loud and annoying. They may exhibit signs of being withdrawn or slouch and not give you eye contact. The point is that there is no set rule to show that a person has low confidence, but each person shows it in different ways. You do too and it is not helping your fear at all.

- Do you bite your nails?

- Do you tap your feet when waiting for something?

- Do you have a low patience threshold?

- Do you put too much of who you are into your work?

You need to recognize the signs and adjust your behavior, because it is turning into something self-destructive rather than being of any benefit to you. Recognizing these signs in others through observation will really help you.

At home exercise 3

In this exercise, you need to give yourself complete attention. Look at your life. Examine why people are not attracted to you and write down what fears you have. You need to know what these fears are before you can actually do anything about them. This may be any number of things but knowing them really helps you to get to know who you are and why you feel all the insecurities that you do. Next to each of your faults, write down something positive about yourself, because you need to balance good and bad. Often people with self-esteem issues cannot find good things to add and that is something we will begin to work on in the next chapter.

If you want your self-esteem levels to be higher, it means taking away some of your faults by coming up with an equally positive thing about you. We all have faults. We all have things we are fearful of but you are letting them rule your life. Write down what you are fearful of as well, as this helps you to reflect on what these bad feelings are and where they are coming from. Having a journal helps you to air these thoughts out and getting them out of your system is a great idea.

These exercises will help you considerably and should be incorporated into your day to day life because with them, you will see a difference in the way that you approach life and that's when you start to gain confidence.

Chapter 3 – Love and Self-love

Love – real love – is probably one of the most misunderstood concepts in our world – not just these days, but for most of human history. Part of the reason why it is this way is because of the plethora of widely received songs and literature, and other forms of media that have been repeated to us so many times with this sense of need for completion along with the depiction of desperate acts in the name of love to win the affection of the person they are after, like learning how to dance the mashed potato.

What kinds of love do we see in the world? Well let's see, there is being enamored with affection; wanting to shower another with affection and be in the same shower, sharing a mutual captivation for each other. This is often known as young love and it is prized to make last as long as possible. Many people find this or feel this way at some point in their lives, as it is often seen in the beginning stages of relationships. Some call it the honeymoon phase. There is a great sense of care for one another and a desire to show it in various ways like body language with lots of touching, giving compliments or playful banter, among doing things for each other and buying things for one another.

People often see these acts and desires as what love is. Sometimes couples keep the sense of this fresh and alive for a long time in their relationship. For many others though, this begins to wane for some reason. The charm fades a bit and people 'get used to each other.' What often happens is an expectation comes from one another to accept and deal what is ultimately a poor sense of self-esteem, slowly and intimately shared (or not but perhaps noticed) as the relationship progresses.

And if one cannot accept or does not know how to support the other's unbalanced sense of self-esteem, the relationship takes a turn as a break up or if a commitment has been made, the charm seems dim if nonexistent. Some will try to revive the relationship or keep it going by reverting back to times they thought were love that is now 'lost' by showing more affection. The problem with this though is that if the expectation of receiving it back is not fulfilled, the person feels hurt. There may be a tinge of sourness or bitterness and fighting or bickering may occur and increase.

So then while affection may last throughout a relationship naturally for some enchanting folk, it becomes dull or does not last for all relationships, so it cannot be real love. What is it then that those fortunate couples have to make that kind of thing keep going? Why do they make it look so easy? Some people are just lucky I guess.

And then there is infatuation. This sense of love involves, whoa – those two who cannot keep their hands off each other. There is a constant want to be in each other's lives, as often as possible, and they will tend to do very spontaneous and perhaps crazy things to express that want and ensure the other of it. It can be a purely sexual attraction, it can be characteristics of another's personality that one 'falls in love with,' it can be a feeling that one gives another just by being around them, or it can be a combination of them all. (Although the one who loves the other for how they make them feel shows that one is more in love with the feeling than the actual person).

Now believe it or not, some people out there are just naturally spontaneous and crazy, and these people are usually confident too, so they become very attractive. Another person may feel so and want or allow this to happen as well and the two form a relationship. If the second person is naturally this way, then the two have a chance of keeping it together with lots of passion if they do not lose control of the relationship with that much energy bouncing around. If one person in the relationship is or becomes less infatuated with the other, a rift begins to form. One will eventually lose interest and it can happen over any given amount of time, whether immediately or over months on end.

What was considered to be 'love' loses its appeal in the form of a want or need for the other person or at least the parts of them that were attractive; the charm fades, and so the sense of love fades. This cannot be true love then. So what is it? What is the secret? What may be the diamond in the rough?

True love may show up in many ways, but one thing is for certain, and that is that it stays. It stays no matter what. That is what is known as unconditional. No matter the circumstance, the action, or the emotion, a nurturing love is there to welcome it with open arms. It is found in forgiveness, it is found in gratitude and in appreciation. These things make love stay because they provide the environment necessary for it to flourish, and flourish it will as long as it is provided these things.

Of course I must mention now and you will read further on that there come limits to just how far you should allow poor actions from another with these things. You must know your boundaries. You will want to know how much you are able to tolerate before you start to feel the effects of the negativity. If it comes to abusive actions in any form whether physical, mental or emotional, that person committing them is suffering themselves (which is why they are causing or sharing suffering), but even if you are the most temperate, forgiving person, an abusive relationship is no environment for love to grow and so you should avoid being in one. Knowing your limits of tolerance comes with self-respect and confidence.

Forgiveness – that which is giving – for – yourself the love that you deserve and letting go of the incident or person that could not give you that; gratitude – being grateful for who you are at heart and what you have, along with those people you care for and those times that help you to remember it; and appreciation – the amount of value that you recognize and give for every opportunity, no matter how good or bad or normal it appears on the surface, in understanding its true purpose in the bigger picture; all help to tame the fiery attitude of righteousness when it comes to getting a healthy sense of self-respect and confidence. This is how you may maintain any form of relationship or partnership; it does not necessarily signify a romantic one (love of affection), but in this way all types are highly rewarding in different ways.

Do you want to know the secret to the secret? It is one that lies right under our noses. If you want to have this, you must be the source of it. Confidence, a healthy self-esteem, personal passion: you are looking for a way to gain or regain these things, so obviously everything that comes with these has got to start with you. And when you cultivate it for yourself, you will attract it in many different ways. It must come from you. You must first familiarize yourself with unconditional love and nurture yourself with it to know what it is like. This is how practicing being comfortable alone can be so beneficial. Then with the confidence of not only knowing it but being it, bit by bit, you draw it to you in amazing ways and you can show it to others without fear of losing it or not having it returned, because you will have made love stay for yourself. It will always be there for you because you will come to know how to treat yourself well and be compassionate no matter what mistakes you make or what emotions you feel. This is true self-love.

If there is only one thing that you take away from reading this book, let it be this: you are already whole. You already possess within you all the things you need to make you feel satisfied and complete. Any sense of longing or incompletion and the need to fill yourself with stuff outside of you is a reflection of something that you have simply forgotten you already have or have yet to discover within yourself. This is what life becomes about – discovering these treasures that make you a whole and complete person and then sharing them with the world for others to enjoy along with you. This is a sense of true love, so if you seek it, look within.

Exercise in self-love – This is going to seem strange to you at first but treat yourself to a long soak in the bath with scented bathwater, or if this does not appeal, how about a facial? If you can't afford one, try using a homemade recipe from the Internet. You need to treat yourself to some small thing every day, even if that's just five minutes' peace and quiet. Write down in your journal what your treat for the day was and feel good about it because you are entitled to have things within your life that are positive and are just for you. It's your life.

Chapter 4 – Adding Boundaries to Your Life

You may be wondering what this has to do with self-esteem and confidence building, but it has everything to do with it. Boundaries are important in life and they allow us to live in harmony with ourselves and in harmony with others. If you were to observe a very happy and balanced person, you would see that this was a person who had sensible rules within his/her life that allow happiness to be a constant thing. For example, a happy and balanced person may not accept certain behaviors are being something that he/she allows. That makes perfect sense. Here are a few areas where boundaries are vital to your happiness and to your self-esteem:

- People need to give you equal respect
- People around you should respect your privacy
- People should respect that you have an opinion
- People should not have unacceptable expectations of you

People with self-esteem problems tend to blur the lines of what's acceptable and what is not. They allow people to take them for granted because they expect to be treated in this way, but until you learn to change your view and set boundaries, you will always have this problem. If people are being rude to you or behaving in a way that upsets you, then this is where boundaries come in. When parents are bringing up children, they give those children guidelines to live by. For example:

- A child is not allowed to play with fire

- A child may be discouraged from going through a parent's handbag

- A child may be asked to leave the room when adults need to talk

These are all reasonable expectations that adults have of children and children should not question them, but as they grow up, the way that they interact with others is determined by the boundaries that they impose just like parents would impose boundaries for their children. These are safeguards and keep people around you in check so that they don't disrespect you and show the world how you expect people to act toward you. Those with self-esteem problems tend to drop their expectations and they shouldn't because boundaries are always important. In fact, without them, friendships fall apart – people don't know where they stand with others and without boundaries relationships fall apart.

If you are married, for example, typical boundaries would be:

- I expect you to be faithful to me
- I expect to be faithful in return
- I expect you to be supportive
- I expect you to stick by me when I need you

These are all reasonable expectations but they form boundaries that are clear:

- You won't be unfaithful
- I won't be unfaithful
- You will not side with others against me

Boundaries are where acceptable behavior resides and when someone steps outside of those boundaries, and then the relationship will ultimately fail.

In order to keep your self-esteem and confidence at a high level, you should write down the relationships that you have and work out what any of those people that are important to you do that makes you very unhappy. There can be all kinds of things that can make you unhappy, but when you actually work them out, you will find that many of them stem from unclear boundaries.

In the workplace, do you know when to stand up for yourself or do you just do as everyone expects you to do? People with self-esteem issues often do things that they don't want to do because they feel that they must, but that adds to their self-esteem issues. In the next chapter we will concentrate on saying "No" but for this chapter, let's look closely at boundaries and what they mean because you need to recognize what are acceptable boundaries and what are not.

From the moment that you are a child, your parents teach you things that you are allowed to do and those things that you are not. The reasons that they do this are to keep you safe from harm. Do not touch the electrical wires – Do not go too close to the fire – Do not leave your shoelaces undone.

As you can see, these are reasonable things that parents place as boundaries upon their children which are positive things and which keep them from hurting themselves. Parents are naturally protective of their children and everyone knows the rights and wrongs that their moms and dads taught them.

As you grew up, you may have had to put up with things that for others would seem unacceptable. Your sister gets all the attention. You brother doesn't respect your privacy. Your sister borrows your things without asking and your school friends get you to do their homework, but do very little in exchange.

We know that low self-esteem comes from feeling not good enough and that it may stem from unhealthy relationships or from things that people have said repeatedly and which stuck. "You are not good enough," or "you are lazy" or "you are ugly" are all things that can stick in your mind and warp your judgment of yourself. Then it follows that if you think yourself unworthy of better treatment, you allow people to step all over your boundaries because you don't think you are important enough to have boundaries. This is of course nonsense.

In every life, an individual needs boundaries. They can be the following with friends:

- At what time is it too late to call?
- How much are you prepared to listen to a negative friend?
- How much criticism are you going to put up with?
- How much are you going to let friends use you?
- How much respect is exchanged between you?

I remember seeing someone with self-esteem issues who had no real boundaries. People would ring her up with their problems after she had gone to bed and she was losing sleep because of it. Then the same friends would criticize her for always being tired. The same friends would ask her to babysit at a moment's notice and expect her to give her time to them without hesitation and there was no mutual respect.

When she was able to address these issues, life became a lot richer. She made it clear that she would take the phone off the hook at bedtime, that she needed notice if they wanted her to babysit for them and when these same people criticized her, she learned to see that they did this to make themselves feel better. Her life changed when she introduced boundaries and no one used her as a doormat any more.

In you relationships with a lover, the same thing has to apply. Let me cite an example from someone with low self-esteem:

- He doesn't let me go to work
- He always looks at other women when we are out together
- He insults me in front of his friends
- He leaves clothes lying around and expects me to pick them up
- He won't help with the housework
- He leaves me to pay for the drinks

The problem in a case like this is that self-esteem is the reason why she puts up with such bad behavior. She thinks she is not entitled to better treatment but of course, everyone is. When a course of action was explained to her that introduced boundaries bit by bit, her boyfriend was actually quite humble and complied and their relationship became stronger. Had she carried on in the same way, he would have left her. She always feared that but what she didn't know was that she gained more respect rather than less by saying enough was enough.

They communicated about why she needed work. It wasn't for the money. He felt he was the provider and felt threatened each time that she mentioned work because it actually felt to him that she was questioning his ability to provide. When she explained it properly and said that she needed intellectual stimulation and just wanted to work to meet people and to keep her happy, he wasn't so negative about it. The insults stopped because she put her foot down in private and said that he should have more respect for her and that unless he did, she was leaving.

As for the housework, she drew up a list of all the things that she had to do and said that he needed to share a little of the load. Because he was a fairly macho kind of guy, she worded it in such a way that he saw this as his protective duty toward her. Their relationship survived but many don't. However, sometimes the relationship has to end to put an end to the behavior which fuels what would be seen as abuse – behavior that is unacceptable and that gives the underdog the feeling that she doesn't count.

In all relationships, there are boundaries and if they are not made clear, it can affect how people treat you and you are likely to be treated unfairly. Why? Because people don't have any idea that what they are doing is unsatisfactory. You have always allowed it – so they have the impression that it's normal for you to be treated in this way.

Only **YOU** can make a difference. Only **YOU** can stop people from using you as a doormat if you don't put up boundaries.

Exercise in Making Boundaries

I want you to look at your existing relationships and if it's a little hard, just take one at a time. Work out what that person does that you find hurts you or makes you unhappy. It could be something like this:

Jennifer expects me to babysit all the time

Jack expects me to clean up his mess at work

You need to correct that activity. In the case of Jennifer, make yourself otherwise occupied and say "No." It's really hard for stressed people with self-esteem issues to do that, but we have you covered in another chapter. However, it's essential that you do. People use you because you allow them to and there is no one to blame but you.

In the case of Jack, look at what your work is and stay within your job description. If you are asked to clear up after another employee, tell them that you really don't have the time to do that. Point blank refuse and tell them it's time they organized their work in a better way so that it does not involve you all the time.

Chapter 5 – Learning to Say "No"

This has a chapter all of its own because it's a very important aspect of finding your own self-respect. Toxic friends have a habit of using people and someone with low self-esteem tries harder to keep friends, so they tend to comply whether it's reasonable or not. I knew of one woman who was so downtrodden that she allowed friends to manipulate her to such an extent that she felt like a servant. That isn't right. In fact, when I asked her why she didn't say "no" the fact was that she was afraid to say "no" and found it easier mentally to do everything they asked her to do. Her friends, in the meantime, took her for granted and used her to such an extent that she diminished her own importance. If you have ever felt completely used up by people, then you will understand this concept. People with self-esteem issues always seek approval. They need to be validated and when they go out of their way to help people, they do it for this validation, but it doesn't really make them feel good long term, because they are too weary to feel good.

So how do you learn to say "No?"

You need to analyze what you do in the period of a normal week. The most important aspects are as follows:

- How much time spent enjoying life with friends?
- How much me time?
- How much time do you have to actually do things for you?
- How much of your time is spent on obligations to others?

Here's a typical week of a twenty five year old with self-esteem issues. She lives alone though she has a small child. She is a single mom and struggles to make ends meet. She listed this in a note pad and doing yours in this way will help you:

Take neighbors kids to school

Pick up kids from school

Do cleaning job – 5 hours a day – 5 days a week

Babysit for friends – 3 night a week

Laundry and cleaning – 2 hours a day

Shopping – for self and friends – 2 hours a day

From this first amount of things that she wrote, it was obvious that a pattern was emerging. She was not just living her life and looking after her own child, but her friends were using her to raise their kids too and they were not giving any of their time in exchange. There was not much social contact for her. She didn't sleep well and had to be up early every day. Her cleaning work was exhausting and she never really had much time for herself.

The problem was that she didn't know how to say "no."

When we introduced hours that were to be devoted to her, she found this very hard at first. We also asked her to say "no" several times a week to obligations for friends. She worried about that because she was concerned that everyone depended upon her, but that was part of the trouble. She didn't know how to say "no" and the only value that she derived for herself out of life was by doing things for other people. She didn't like herself very much and had real self-esteem issues. Thus, she never treated herself to time for her that was essential to her wellbeing.

Ways to say "no"

We explained to her that she had to learn to say no, and that there were several ways that she could do this. One of these was to be honest and tell the friend that she had other plans. Another was to think of something more important that she had to do. For example, she had dental appointments that stopped her from collecting other people's kids and enlisted the help of people who would have to pick up their kids anyway.

By the end of a fortnight, she was able to allocate a certain amount of time for herself that she had not had for a very long time. This is very important. If you don't like yourself, you need time to develop your own inner feelings for yourself. Give yourself a nice treat like a new haircut, make yourself look nice or simply have an evening or afternoon relaxing without having to think of obligations to other people. By gradually incorporating "me" time, she was actually surprised when her kids mentioned how much happier she seemed to be and that added to her self-esteem and helped her to find her way out of the vicious circle she had put herself into.

There are several ways that you can say "no," When you know that a friendship is not on an equal give and take basis, you do need to learn to say "no" and wait for the relationship to become more solid with something in it for everyone. Otherwise, you begin to feel used and feel your low self-esteem.

It is vital that you recognize problems and that you handle them as and when they present yourself. What you need to write down is a list of all the people that you know. Then beside each name – work out how much you give to the relationship and be honest and appraise how much you get given back.

Jennifer	Good longtime friend	Give and take equally
Susan	Newish neighbor	Takes me for granted
John	Friend from work	Piles on the work

Thus, your list will dictate which people need adjustment to the way that they behave toward you. If there is less than 50 50 give and take, then you need to even the score a little by learning to say "no." People won't think worse of you for doing it. Initially, you may feel a little guilt because you are accustomed to being used, but that's very different from the long term effects, which are that people start to gain respect for you.

Saying "No" is as simple as that, but you can do it in a friendly manner. Remember to treat people how you would like to be treated. If there are any toxic friends among your list, you need to have as little contact with these people as possible. Then look at the friendships where you give a lot but seem to get very little back. If the friendship is worth keeping for you, then even out the score by being busy sometimes when they ask you to help out. You need time to yourself. You also need to be able to dictate the course of your own life, rather than having other people do it all of the time.

The only way forward out of this chain of events is to have free time to yourself, to pamper yourself a little bit and to allow yourself the luxury of learning to love yourself. That always sounds a little odd, but if you don't love you, how can others love you? Thus, use the time you gain to do things that make you feel good about yourself and build up positivity. Try yoga if you want to, or try joining a night class or a gym. Do something for you.

Chapter 6 – Why Saying "No" Makes a Difference to Self-Esteem

It has been made fairly obvious in the last chapter why people need to say no, but perhaps you haven't seen the link between being able to say "no" and self-esteem. Imagine the scenario that is shown below and it will become clearer to you. This is a hypothetical situation but it could well happen and it's important for you to see how people using you actually means that you respect yourself less and are respected less by other people.

Molly works five days a week. At the weekend, she wants to spend time with her husband. Her husband, however, thinks that playing golf is more important and spends most of the weekend doing this. She understands that this is a hobby of his and appreciates that he needs some time for hobbies. However, whenever she suggests that they have time together, her husband puts her down and says that she is too needy. This makes her feel worthless. She was told as a child that she was not very good at things and has taken this notion into her married life. Thus, what he says goes. Add to that they have three children. She spends every weekend looking after the kids while he is out. When he gets back, he expects his dinner to be on the table and his washing to be done and ironed ready for work the next week.

Molly has neighbors who use her as a doormat. The next door neighbor is always asking her to run errands and she has gotten so used to doing them that they are now part of her life. Instead of thanking her when she does an errand, the neighbor always finds fault and reinforces that Molly is pretty stupid and has no value. Thus, she goes through life feeling like she isn't worth much. At work, even though she has been at the company longer than anyone else, she finds she is left behind when it comes to promotion. Why? Because she isn't very good at delegating and would rather do the work herself than cause ripples. Thus, people at work make her feel inadequate as well. Altogether, her life is very unhappy and she has no self-esteem.

What Molly could do to make her life better:

Ask family and friends to help with the kids, to give her a little free time.

Learn to play golf and show her husband she's very good at it or alternate with her husband so that he gets golf one day and he gets to look after the kids on the other day so that she gets time to do things that she wants to do.

In her workplace situation, she needs to be harder but also needs to face the fact that people treat her the way that they do because she has given the impression that it's ok to treat her badly. She needs to start delegating and to feel good about her work. She needs to learn when to say "No" and when to be too busy to help others.

Molly has the potential that anyone else has to be happy. However, she puts herself last all the time and when you do that to yourself, you tend to see yourself as having very little importance. That's where the link comes in. By allowing people to use you all the time, you have little mental energy left to energy left to actually enjoy life. When you learn to balance your life and start to look after yourself, you begin to see your mistakes and it's only your mistakes that are leaving you feeling so used and miserable.

This can become a very vicious circle that is hard to get out of, but it's not impossible. Think about tomorrow. Think about what YOU want to achieve and how much time you can free up to let yourself enjoy life. Your enjoyment can be very simple indeed. You may want to go for a walk in the park. You may want to join a local yoga class. You may want to paint pictures or do something creative. Don't belittle those ideas. You only get one life and if you deny yourself choice in life, you will continue to have self-esteem issues and will never really feel happy.

Changing bad habits is essential. You can feel good about yourself in different ways. Do you look nice? Do you have something you can wear that will make you look nice? Do you feel tired and restless or find that long term relationships don't work out very well? The thing is that you only have one life and every moment of it that you waste on being unhappy about yourself is a moment lost. You need to learn to enjoy yourself and look after yourself, which is why I have devoted the next chapter to ways in which you need to change your life for the better.

There is no time like the present and now is also the time to realize that whatever people say to you says more about them than it does about you. If people are unkind to you, it shows that they are unkind people. If they are rude to you, then this makes them a lesser person than you because rudeness isn't a good trait to have. Stop beating yourself up because others are doing this. That's their problem. To begin to take your life in control, you need to realize that you cannot be judged by what people say, but you will certainly be judged about how you let people stamp all over you.

Exercise in saying "No"

There are two ways you could do this exercise. You could face up to someone and say "no" the next time an unreasonable demand is made, or you can make yourself busy and unavailable to them so that you don't have to. Either way, you have to get out of this habitual saying "yes" to people that you want to say "no" to.

To make yourself feel better, be more available to friends where the relationship is two way. Recognize good friendships and give to them in favor to giving to relationships that are not on an equal footing. You have to recognize that if you say "no" the world will not stop turning. You will feel bad for a short while because of guilt. Bake a cake for a neighbor and do something positive to get rid of that guilt. It works.

Chapter 7 - Mind, Spirit, Soul – Looking After You

In other chapters, you have learned about how to relax. However, in this chapter, we are talking about how important it is that mind, spirit and soul are intact at all times. They cannot be if you continue to have self-esteem problems. Let's take these one at a time and try to show you how to improve your lot in life:

Mind

Your mind is something that you control. If you have bleak thoughts and are unhappy, that's just because you choose to look at the world in a very negative way. If you look at a cripple in a wheelchair, you may be surprised to see how happy he is. It's not about your state of body. It's not about your capabilities. It's about the way that you take care of yourself and see the world around you. If you are overtired, for example, you have to start listening to your mind. Perhaps you are not getting enough sleep. Many people who have self-esteem issues don't because they are too busy with their negativity to actually be able to get off to sleep at night. Your mind needs three things:

Adequate food – Adequate rest – Adequate water – Adequate exercise

You may think that these are not important but they are the most important elements of your life. Many people with self-esteem issues neglect their health and that's the worst thing that you can do. You need breakfast to wake yourself up ready for another day. You need to feed your mind by reading regularly and the morning newspaper is okay for this so why not treat yourself to time in the morning to appreciate the world, to eat your breakfast and catch up on the latest news. At lunch, eat a balanced diet, and make sure that you drink plenty of water because although you may not think of it, it's equally as important as the food that you eat. Let's tell you what happens when you don't eat and drink sufficiently.

Your body gets tired if it does not get the nutrients that it needs. You may already be depressed, stressed or have problems with self-esteem. If you don't eat the right foods, the stress levels get higher, you can develop illness and thus the vicious circle begins to happen. You feel worse and your body is crying out for the right foods.

Similarly, it may not be obvious to you that you are not drinking enough water. You may drink coffee or tea and think that's enough water, but it's a totally different thing. If you do not drink water, the following happens:

- Muscles get dehydrated

- You can get cramps

- Your skin and hair gets out of condition

- Your digestive system does not work correctly

Imagine yourself with self-esteem or stress problems and then add the water problem and you begin to look ill and notice that your skin and hair are not looking their best. Worst of all, you are dehydrating your body or depriving it of the water it needs for normal function.

Exercise in inspiration– You may wonder what this has to do with mind, body and soul and it has everything to do with it. If you were to lie in bed all day every day, eventually your muscles would give you problems, you would get stiff and you would put on weight or even make yourself very ill indeed. Even people who are bedbound need exercise and for them there is little alternative but to doing exercises with a physiotherapist. If you are stressed and you do not burn energy, you feel sluggish and unable to deal with problems and this adds to your stress.

Mind and body need to work together and your soul comes into the picture when you think about wholeness and feeling good about yourself. People who are spiritual are less likely to feel the weight of stress or the burden of having self-esteem issues. Take the time and go to a beauty spot and walk a little. Look at what it is that awe inspires you because this will be different for everyone. The reason that mindfulness is useful because it helps you to notice things and when you start to waken your spirit to what is happening around you, you tend not to internalize so much, so you are able to get away from stressful thoughts.

When you find somewhere that awe inspires you, look at it with new eyes. Try to clear all thoughts out of your head and just see what it is that brings out that awe. Feel small, because that's good for you. Humility isn't a bad thing ever. Feel close to your God whoever that is and begin to build up a picture of that inspirational scenery in your mind. Take in everything that you see and build it as a memory in your mind, because this will be useful. Whenever you think negative thoughts about yourself or anything else, close your eyes and see that awe again, because sometimes you need to be reminded of the scale of things. If you have a picture of it in your mind, it's easy to grab hold of it when you need to and that makes your soul feel very much at peace.

You may not know this but your subconscious needs room to work. When you are stressed, you don't give it the room that it needs. Remember how you lost those keys and then when you were not thinking about it, you suddenly remembered where they were? This is because your subconscious was able to work on the problem once you put it out of your mind. It is the same when you are stressed. Your subconscious can't help you because you haven't given it the space it needs. You are drowning it with bad thoughts or with stressful thoughts. Learn to let go, and let your subconscious do the work that it was intended that it should do and you will feel a sense of wellbeing that you haven't felt for a long time.

Exercise in eating – When you sit down to eat, taste every bite. People are too quick to swallow and don't take the time to taste all the textures, the flavors and appreciate the foods that they are eating. For the next meal, make sure you have time to sit down and savor every taste you eat. When you practice mindfulness in everything, you begin to appreciate the moment more.

Exercise in drinking water – If you really don't like plain water, and many people don't, try drinking it with a cordial and avoid all the modern foods that have so many additives and colorings that they may be harming who you are. Avoid soda, avoid those drinks that are heavy in sugar and start to appreciate water because the goodness that it will do for your body will help your soul to feel happier and your body to feel cared for. You may not think that it makes a lot of difference, but it really does. Try to drink 8 glasses of water a day. That's vital to feeling good and making the most of your body.

Exercise in movement and posture

When people take up yoga, they are actually surprised when they are told that posture is the all important aspect of yoga that counts more than anything else. How can sitting straight change things? It changes things from several viewpoints. Your body language changes when you care about your posture. You no longer look timid and people are less likely to take advantage of you. Why it's so important to mind, body and soul is that you have energy centers within the body and if your posture is off, then energy flow through the body may also be off.

Even if you do not believe in that, you have to admit that different people give off different body language. Look at someone confident and sure of themselves and you will see someone who is generally upright and doesn't slouch. Lazy people tend to slouch and those who are aggressive or nervous will show even different body language. For someone who has self-esteem issues, it is worthwhile paying attention to the way that you sit, the way that your body gives out a language of its own and the way that your energy flow works.

Thus, stand in front of a mirror in the normal position you would have when you walk into a room. Now, try to hold your shoulders back, your head higher with your back straight and your arms by your side and walk into the room again. You instantly boost what you look like and people are less likely to take you for granted if you have good posture.

Now, try something else. Try keeping your back straight and your tummy in and see how you feel after a day. Posture is so important. When you walk or move, try to be conscious of what position you are in because the energy needs to flow through your body. When it does, you are less likely to feel stressed and more likely to feel energized.

Recommendations

If you can possibly afford it, take up yoga classes. People who do learn all about feeling the goodness from within. They learn to breathe in a particular way that helps them to gain energy and confidence. You may think this is a fad but it's been going on for thousands of years and there's a very good reason for it. Yoga helps people to become more relaxed. It also works on your confidence and energy levels so that you feel much more energy in your life and if you have self-esteem issues, or are stressed, it's the perfect way to get close to who you really are and discover the best part of being you.

I would recommend that you find a good beginner's class where you are comfortable with the teacher, as this really will help you to become more confident of yourself and help you to unwind as well. Yoga really can help you with all of those types of things.

Chapter 8 – Learning About Your Good Points

We have touched on negative things, and perhaps you were not confident enough to see your own good points. Let's create a few so you can start to feel good about who you are. It helps your interaction with others if you do something out of the ordinary, which is positive.

Exercise in positivity 1

In this exercise, do something for someone else that you do not usually do. For example, you could bake a cake for an elderly neighbor and go and give it to her. There are all manner of things that you can do to help your positivity levels and to feel good about yourself. Telephone a friend you have not talked to in a while and discipline yourself to only be positive regardless of how bad you feel. This is a great exercise for cheering someone else up. If people are accustomed to you being negative, then this helps you to re-establish positive contacts with people.

Write a letter to a friend you have not seen for a while or try something artistic or creative. Creative things are great for bringing out the best in a person. Making a homemade birthday card for a friend is positive. Scrapbooking all those old photographs is positive. Cleaning out the mucky drawer in the kitchen is positive. Do not overdo it. Just try to add a positive action for each of the negatives that you wrote about yourself in the last exercise. As you do, cross out one negative for each positive because as you do, you will begin to feel better about who you are.

If you really think yourself guilty of being so bad and so negative, call these exercises 'paying your dues' and use them to reduce all the negative thoughts you have about yourself. Positive interactions and actions really do go a long way to make people feel better about themselves. Remember though that you must never let yourself be used by people. The actions that you take to make yourself feel better about your life must be your choice, rather than being tasks that others impose on you. You are not someone else's doormat.

Exercise in self-indulgence

It is time that you indulged yourself a little. If you have been weary of life for a while and feel that your confidence levels are low, you need to treat yourself to something that makes you feel good. It could be a haircut. It could be a change of style. It could even be something that you feel good about doing. Learn that you are worth treating because you are. If you do not have excess cash, it does not have to be something expensive. Allow yourself a little luxury in life. A nice shampoo or a bubble bath can work just as well as any other kind of spa treatment, if you allow yourself the indulgence. Simply going for a 15 minute walk has shown to do wonders for people's self-esteem. It gets you outside where there is fresher air and movement. It allows you to air out the thoughts in your mind and become more involved in your surroundings to help you feel more connected. Doing this on a consistent basis will show significant results for you over time.

Try to think of this as a special date with yourself. For a while now, you have not given yourself the treats in life because your self-confidence is low. Now is a time to put that right and to enjoy your treat with all your senses. If you delight in eating fresh strawberries, then enjoy them to the fullest. Taste the fruit, feel the texture on your tongue and think of nothing else but treating yourself.

Similarly, in a bathtub with bubble bath, soak away your worries and use your mind and your senses to enjoy the moment. When you lack confidence, often you forget to treat yourself and if you use your senses to enjoy the moment, as is the case in mindfulness practice, you actually give yourself a real positive boost.

I can tell you from personal experience that I used to take on stress so much that it even prevented me from enjoying the things I actually love to do like learning, writing, drawing, and riding my bike. I lost confidence in myself and lost the enthusiasm to pursue the things that gave me personal pleasure. I would even try to do these things regardless because I told myself that the enthusiasm would come back, and as I did I realized that under the stress I had turned my entire life into a state of just going through the motions.

When it came to things that would occupy a majority of my time like college, work, and household chores, I would begrudgingly anticipate the next thing to come with the attitude of "let's just get this over with." The hope was that once I was through with these obligations, I could give my time to treating myself to the things I really enjoyed doing. However, it became apparent that my blasé attitude bled into the rest of my life since I maintained that attitude for the majority of my time anyways. The things I enjoyed doing became a practice of just going through the motions because in a subtle yet substantial way, I had desensitized myself from being fully engaged in any activity in order to protect myself from the constant stress I felt.

Luckily I have been able to turn that around, and even if your story does not completely resonate with mine, you can turn yourself around to get the most out of your life again too. That is why when I tell you to use all of your senses to enjoy the moment, I mean that you should stay aware of as much of the experience that you can to get the most out of it. Most of the time this means taking things slow. Do not rush yourself as you may be used to doing in other areas of your life. The slower your pace in self-indulgence, they more time you give yourself to take in as much that your indulgence of choice has to offer. This is what mindfulness and expansion of awareness is all about. This is exactly what it means to stay present; to stay in the moment. What better way to cultivate this than by doing the things that you love and truly interest you!

It is not wrong to look after yourself. People who lack confidence often do not feel they deserve treats but they are every bit as entitled to treats as anyone else it. Most often they are so used to putting others before themselves with a caring attitude, or they have been trained to think that they must work themselves to the bone before they can reap rewards from it, or they have become so used to the feeling of neglect or being put down that they forget their own value and how to show themselves appreciation for that value. Self-nourishment is a foreign and forlorn concept to them.

Pleasurable moments in your life add to your sense of positivity as long as they do not involve guilt. For example, if you are overweight, you do not get that great feeling by indulging in something that makes your problem worse. An overweight person may be working hard at getting healthy by changing their diet and exercising and reach a point where they see some success, so they decide to reward themselves with some candy, a greasy burger, or an ice cream sundae. They know that this reward is counterproductive to all the effort they have been putting in, but they do it anyways because they really want it.

They are feeding into an old guilty craving, and they can try to convince themselves that this one moment will be ok, but it opens the door to falling back down the slippery slope of the self-depreciative state that they had come from. You can consider an act like this as 'eating the guilt.' Choose a treat that is special but one that will not add guilt to your negativity. Make your treat something that does not have to do with the negativity you are healing from. For example if you are used to coping with your negativity by indulging in food and you have been working to counteract that, reward yourself with something other than food, like going to a movie. If you are used to coping with stress by withdrawing yourself from social environments, reward yourself by taking up a hobby that you have always had interest in but never gave the time to practice.

In the next chapter, we are going to deal with relaxation. People who are stressed and anxious usually find it difficult to relax. Their thought processes do not let them get the rest that they need. Be prepared to switch this mode off because the next chapter insists on it and it is good for you to know how.

For the time being, go over this chapter again and make sure that you observe the two exercises outlined in this chapter as they are helpful for you to make your way to emotional freedom and freedom from self-confidence and self-esteem issues.

Chapter 9 – Relaxation

Do you know when panic sets in? You feel that horrible feeling that you cannot breathe and people tell you the trick about breathing into a paper bag. What this does is help you to concentrate more on your breathing, and you become more engaged in it by having to focus on the visual representation of the bag expanding and contracting. Panic attacks in high anxiety situations cause you to hyperventilate, which leaves you short of breath. Without getting enough oxygen to nourish your cells, carbon dioxide accumulates in your body that causes physical stress, adding to the mental stress you are already feeling.

By breathing in used air within the paper bag, you calm your body down and of course it works in a panic situation. However, people who feel anxiety and fear need to know what it is like to relax and often do not remember how. They do not rest their minds. They do not rest their body and often lose sleep because of the way that they feel. You need to learn relaxation methods because these help you to get out of a funk and breathe correctly so that your body does not go into panic state when things happen that are unexpected.

Relaxation Exercise to Help You with Your Breathing

The idea of this exercise is to help you find a peaceful place within yourself so that you can give your mind a rest. This is necessary because people who feel fear do so because thoughts get too large in their heads and make situations even more stressful than they really are.

Choose a bedroom in your house where you can have uninterrupted time. You should turn off outside stimulation like noises from the TV and choose a time when there are not kids making a noise in the house. This is time that you need for yourself. Lie down on the bed and make sure that you loosen all clothing, so as not to be constricted in any way. Make sure that a pillow to help optimize breathing supports your head. It works well if you have a room which is slightly shaded, so closing the curtains to the outside world may help you to be less distracted.

Close your eyes. Place your hands onto your body just beneath the chest. Breathe in through the nose and hold the breath for several seconds. Then breathe out and feel your upper abdomen pushing the air out through your mouth. To make sure that you are breathing properly, you should feel the space just below your ribcage expand outward as you inhale. This is where your diaphragm is located. It is the true muscle for breathing, and as it expands it fills your lungs with air. Breathing from your diaphragm as opposed to your chest or throat helps to fill the total volume of your lungs, getting more oxygen into the blood system that nourishes each and every cell in your body, helps you feel more relaxed, and eliminates stress. Carry on doing this for several moments. Five to ten minutes would be optimal. While you are breathing, concentrate solely on the breath going into your body, holding it and then breathing out. Think of nothing else.

Relaxation exercise 2 – Giving Your Body and Mind a Break

Using the same lying down position as you did for your breathing exercise, this time you are going to give your mind a total rest from worries to make you feel less likely to feel panic and fear. When you mind and body are rested, you begin to feel stronger and more able to face up to situations that may have, in the past, given you cause for fear. In this exercise, you are asked to be aware of each part of your body in turn. Close your eyes and keep them closed for the whole of the exercise. You will need about 20 minutes for this exercise.

Imagine your toes. Think of them; focus on feeling them tense up. Then relax them and feel your toes relaxing. They may give the impression of being heavy and that is good. Once that part of your body is totally relaxed, continue to think of the next area of your body, i.e. the ankles, then the calves, then the knees, then the thighs etc. until your whole body is relaxed. During the course of this exercise, think of nothing else. Think only of the part of your body, on tensing it and then letting it relax.

People who relax sufficiently are able to sleep better and thus become stronger because sleep is necessary for good health. Though you may not be aware of it, your body is healing while you sleep and that is important for your mind as well as your body. Relaxation also helps you to cope with life in a better way so that when a fear arises, you can simply breathe correctly until the fear has passed, rather than going into a panic.

Of course, there will be things that make you afraid, but your response will become different and you will no longer see the fears that you have as being threatening. You will be able to cope better with them because your mind has relaxed and is all fresh and ready to meet whatever fear comes your way.

Exercise to use when faced with panic

Be aware of the moment. Breathe in through your nose and out through your mouth. If you control your breathing and concentrate solely upon it, the moment will pass. There are all kinds of reasons why people feel afraid, but hyperventilating makes fear grow and it is that out-of-control feeling that you are trying to control with your breathing. Breathe in through the nose, hold the breath for a moment and then breathe out of your mouth. It is a good idea to practice this in day-to-day situations that may not be frightening, but which may cause stress, so that when it becomes an automatic response to any stress or fear triggers, you will find it helps you to get over that fear.

The reason you are asked to breathe out of your mouth in an instance such as this is because you actually expel more air this way. Normal breathing should be in through the nose and out through the nose, but in this case, you are purposely allowing more of the oxygen to leave your body so that you do not hyperventilate and that's very important. Hyperventilation makes your blood pressure rise and it's actually making you panic even more. You need to control your breathing so that you are in the driving seat of your life, rather than giving in to what's happening around you. These moments of panic will pass and when they do, you may wonder why they caused you such stress. The reason is that you allowed them to. By learning to breathe correctly, you are taking your life into your own control and will find that panics are less frequent.

Chapter 10 – Getting Sufficient Sleep

We have bordered on how important sleep, exercise, drinking water and eating the right foods are but sleep is one area where more and more people tend to deprive themselves, especially when feeling bad about themselves or worked up with stress. Sleep is a very special time for the human body. It's when all the hormones are released that allow your body to heal. It's also a time when you need all the different stages of REM sleep. If you don't have these, eventually you will be too exhausted to help yourself because your mind really does need all the help that it can get to help you through stressful times. You may be one of the increasing numbers of people who say that sleep isn't important to you, but you would be kidding yourself if you think this. It's an excuse for not trying and that's really not good enough if you want to find your way to ultimate happiness and peace of mind. In the last chapter, we talked about relaxation but sleep is one stage further and you are going to have to make an effort to achieve it. There are several things that you can do to help yourself and we have outlined these in this chapter.

Bedroom

The bedroom should be geared to sleeping. The temperature within the room should be comfortable. Often people close off bedrooms and they get stuffy and air is necessary in a space where you are going to sleep. The best way to do this is to open the windows in the daytime to air the room but close them at night, so that you are not cold. The bedroom should be a very relaxing place. Your bed needs to be comfortable. You also need to have clean sheets and a comfortable pillow. Many people struggle all night with an uncomfortable pillow and it's not surprising that they cannot sleep. The bedroom should be a place of calmness. Thus, if you tend to get out of bed and use the computer, you need to rehouse this in another room so that your bedroom is strictly used for sleeping.

Your mind

Your mind will be better equipped for sleep if you do not watch violent television late at night. Get yourself ready for bed and that includes the way that your mind is working. Thus, it's far better to have peaceful activities before bedtime. Reading, doing the crossword and allowing yourself to slow down naturally is the best way to prepare for bedtime.

Food

Your digestion needs to work correctly and if you eat directly before bedtime, it's going to disturb your sleep because the digestion process has just begun. Thus make sure that you do not eat just before bedtime and that you are ready for bed by drinking a malted drink that is suitable for bedtime. Anything such as coffee or tea is a stimulant and will keep your mind wide awake. Thus, avoid these after about 7 in the evening.

Exercise to help you to sleep

You may have heard that people count sheep and there's a very good reason why they do. However, sheep are hardly relevant to day to day life unless you live in the country and if you do, then I don't think you would be looking in a book for solutions to self-esteem and stress as these tend to be more prevalent in a hectic lifestyle. So, you need to find something to help you to sleep, which is more relevant.

If you drive, this will be perfect. When you lie in bed at night, close your eyes and be ready to sleep. Turn off the light. Relax for a few moments. It's quite likely that you are kept awake by thoughts. Thus, if we replace those thoughts with something for you to concentrate on, that may work. It does for many. Thus imagine getting into your car. Imagine the drive from your house to somewhere very familiar, somewhere where you know the roads off by heart. Imagine everything that you do when you drive, such as placing the key in the ignition, what you do with the pedals, what you can see out of the window. I remember one friend trying this out and she had in mind to drive from her house to town. She got as far as the end of the road and then fell asleep and asked why that happened. The thing is that you are replacing the thoughts that go around in your head with something that your mind is accustomed to doing almost as if it's automatic. Thus, if you give it something to do, it doesn't need to chase thoughts.

Often people who have self-esteem issues or have stress in their lives overthink things and this is particularly true when they go to bed. If you tried to go to bed and think of nothing, you would fail. The reason for this is fairly obvious. What happens is that you are asking your mind to do something it is unaccustomed to doing and it will fight you every step of the way. Instead of doing that, give it something alternative to think about and concentrate fully. If you find that your thoughts start wandering, go back to the starting line again and begin your driving experience all over again until you start to get the hang of it.

You are replacing the potential for negative thinking. At the same time, you are giving your subconscious mind a little bit of room to do what it needs to do. Just as the body heals overnight, the mind needs a certain amount of rest too. It is such an easy exercise to do and it helps you to get off to sleep. If you don't drive, think of something that you do that is almost automatic. It may be the laundry or it may even be counting sheep, but whatever it is, use it to help you to stop thinking negative thoughts that feed your self-esteem issues or worries.

Chapter 11 – Meditation and More Breathing

What is so great about meditation and why do we keep hearing about it from so many different sources these days as a beneficial practice? Is everybody turning into a monk or something? Well, while meditation has a long standing history in eastern cultures that practice Buddhism, Hinduism, Taoism and so on, the practice is gaining momentum in the western world in today's society for one main reason – it works.

So how do we familiarize ourselves with meditation? It is true that the concept of meditation can appear vague at first because the practice of it has found so many different venues and taken on so many different forms. There is meditation in the practice of a single activity, a single thought or mantra; meditation on nothing with the aim of clearing our minds completely; and guided meditations that give us visuals to focus on and lead us through a journey in our imagination, just to name a few. Not one of them is particularly considered to be a better practice than the other, however the presence of variations in meditation make it available to suit the needs and preferences of most any individual.

The ultimate goal of any form of meditation is to lessen the volume of unnecessary thoughts that tend to overrun our minds and prevent us from being able to focus. Even if we are engaged in a task, it is quite possible that we have varying other clusters of thoughts running in the background that are ready to jump into the foreground at any given chance, and that can become quite distracting. For matters of low or high self-esteem, these are most often thoughts that repeat in our minds in any given situation that have locked us into a certain perception about ourselves that are actually not true. These thoughts prevent us from being able to stay present in the moment, and indeed keep us from making the most of any opportunity that is given to us because of these preconceived notions.

Have you ever been at a party, wanting to enjoy yourself but your frame of mind keeps you from doing just that? Say for example you see someone interesting across the room that you would like to engage in conversation, but before or while you are even walking across the room to them you begin thinking, "What will I say to them?" or, "How will I make a good impression?" or, "What if I embarrass myself?" These are characteristic of a lower self-esteem persona, and they inhibit you from living out your true desires.

A person with an unhealthy sense of high self-esteem will probably already have what they are going to say scripted in their mind. It is not a bad thing to have an idea of what you will say to a person before you begin a conversation with them, however for this type with what they have scripted in their mind to say there is little room for an organic conversation to grow. It usually acts as a protective barrier for them to steer the conversation so that they will not have to be put on the spot. They gain control by leading others around without having to think about the conduct of their own way of expression.

Someone with a normal sense of self-esteem will notice the person across the room, walk over to them and simply say, "Hello, what is your name?" or verbalize something they noticed about that person that would make for a good ice breaker, or share a thought about the party that they are at that would lead to an open conversation for both people to take a chance at having the floor to talk. This is how an organic conversation develops, and without background thoughts muscling their way into the minds of the people speaking, it opens doors to the spontaneous sharing of ideas, laughter and engagement. In other words, people allow themselves to be free and open to whom they really are which, ideally, is the kind of experience that everyone would like to have. How do you get to this place if you are so used to being barraged by thoughts?

One method to try practicing is meditation on your own time. The more that you practice this by yourself, the more the practice will lend its benefits to you when you are engaging with other people.

Traditional Meditation

Clear your mind. You have probably heard this phrase before. Honestly, most people might be familiar with this expression and not have a clue what it actually feels like because there is always something occupying the space up there. And that is ok. It is what we have been trained to do from young ages – learn this, study that, brush your teeth, have you written out your schedule? Don't forget to go to the grocery store!

And then on top of this cornucopia of checklists and things to do is a layer of thought more important to us – those thoughts about ourselves, our identity, our desires, and our social status: "He/She is really cute, I hope they notice me today;" "I am not going to dress like those people because I have got my own style;" "I want to be living on the coast with the job I love in five years. And maybe I will have a dog. No, a cat, because cats do their own thing." These rambling thoughts that keep our minds so busy pull us away from being able to focus on what actually matters.

Traditional meditation is a practice that has been around for thousands of years. For something to stick around that long that promotes positivity there must be something to it. It must be important enough in some way and developed so well that there is a reason people continue to use it to this day, so let's take a look at how it works. Traditional meditation holds the aim of being able to keep a clear mind as long as possible. Take it from me, this is not as easy as it sounds. It is like trying to find a place without any noise, but still there are almost always car engines in the distance, household machines running, or birds chirping somewhere not too far off. Regardless, it can be done, and with practice you can do well at bringing your mind to this space readily.

Holding a clear mind comes with the ability to stay calm in any circumstance, along with the ability to tune out distractions more effectively so that you can concentrate better on whatever it is you wish to focus. You will also gain a greater understanding of situations from a broader perspective, and respond with your true authentic self as opposed to reacting while emotionally charged or under the guise of some false, preconceived notions.

Traditional Meditation Exercise

While starting out in any type of meditation exercise, it is crucial that you find a quiet place to practice that is free of distractions. Allowing any interruptions in your environment will take away from the quality of your exercise.

Allow yourself 15 minutes for this exercise. You can set a timer if you would like to, and you can always increase the amount of time for this practice as you get more comfortable with it. People who have practiced this meditation for a while will even spend up to one hour doing it, so just keep in mind that it is up to you to find a pace that is right for you.

Find a nice quiet room or space outside. Turn off your phone, computer, television and any other electronic device, or better yet do not even bring them in the room with you. Find a place to sit or lie down comfortably and begin breathing rhythmically. Start out with your normal breathing pattern, and then as you begin to equalize inhaling and exhaling, increase the depth of your breaths until you find a nice rhythm. This will be your only focus for this meditation.

Once you have found a comfortable deep breathing pattern, make sure that you place your focus solely on the breathing and tune out all other thought. This is the beginning of developing a clear mind. Begin to count your breaths, starting with one. For each breath that you count, maintain a clear mind without thought as best you can. Your goal will be to count up to ten, however anytime that a thought enters your mind while you are breathing, you will start the count again at one.

For example, you are breathing, you inhale and count 'one,' and then on the exhale a thought enters your mind, "I am really glad that I am giving myself the time to do this." Now on your next inhale, you will have to count one again. Again, if you inhale and count 'one,' and then exhale and your mind remains as quiet as the room that you are in, on the next inhale you may count to 'two,' and then a thought pops into your head, "I have to pick up Jenny at soccer practice by six o'clock tomorrow." On the next inhale you will have to start at one.

When you first start out doing this, you may find that you have only counted to one many times throughout the entire 15 minutes and did not even get to count to two. That is perfectly ok and actually quite normal. Did I mention that this exercise is a great practice in patience as well? Try to not take it so seriously. Instead, have fun with it and be proud of yourself that you are trying something new that will reward you under any circumstance for the rest of your life. I practiced this technique myself daily for two weeks and by the end of the two weeks, I found that I was only able to count up to three. Be that as it may, I noticed that by the end of the two weeks I could think more clearly, I was more attentive at work and could handle multi-tasking my day with a greater bit of ease. Not to mention that while I would normally feel a bit of stress in trying to manage all that I was doing from day to day, I noticed my regular mood improving too.

Singular Meditation

This type of meditation involves placing all of your focus on a single activity, affirmation, mantra or chant. Our minds are used to doing this anyways and define the mental and physical state we are in by the thoughts and phrases that we repeat constantly. Think about it – how often do you find yourself repeating the same thing in a given situation? You have an interest in art, playing an instrument or a particular sport, and you practice on a regular enough basis, but you do not find yourself improving as you would like to. You feel like you keep hitting a wall, or that you are just not good enough. And this is what you tell yourself, "I am ok at it, but I am not that good." And you repeat this anytime someone asks you how you are doing at it, "I am hanging in there, but I am not great at it." You have set a limit for yourself that you will never be able to move beyond, despite all your efforts, until you change your frame of mind.

How often have you found yourself saying, "I am stress out!" or, "I feel depressed," or, "Nobody understands what I have to deal with." These are hazardous mantras that some of us continue to tell ourselves, aware of a problem because our feelings tell us so, looking for some answer to relieve our grief, without realizing that we are perpetuating the cycle. We feel a certain way, we tell ourselves how or why that is to confirm it, and then our minds are programmed to think that way so when we encounter a situation that makes us feel that way again, we go around in the same cycle confirming it and living it out repeatedly. Many people can live out their entire lives this way without understanding why because as our external environment appears to change, we still feel low since our internal environment has not changed.

Break the cycle! The secret to this plaguing conundrum is that no matter how hopeful or prosperous our external environment appears, whether we are living in a tenement apartment or a mansion, whether we have many friends or just one, only we have control over our own thoughts and feelings. Once you change your way of thinking and convince yourself of the positivity in your life, like magic, you will see the prosperity of your external environment change for the better. The truth is though that nothing externally has actually changed, it is merely reflecting the way you see it, and the way you see the world is determined by how you see yourself.

This change does not happen immediately because what it took for you to get to the point you are at now did not happen overnight. It took a long amount of time with a lot of repetitious thoughts to convince you otherwise, so you must find it within yourself to establish repetitive thoughts that will empower you gracefully and allow yourself the time for those positive repetitive thoughts to take root. That way you can become convinced of your true self – you are an awesome person regardless of what anyone else says or thinks.

Go beyond doubt – if you are trying for positivity and your mind gives you a doubt or an excuse, recognize it but do not give in to it. Even if you do not believe it at the moment, continue to tell yourself, "I am a wonderful person and here is why…" and then find one small thing that you are happy with about yourself and say it. Remember the classic story of the little engine that could – "I think I can, I think I can, I think I can…" It does not matter if it is a book for children, the message is a valid and profound one that holds true for people of all ages and it is never too late to turn yourself around, just stay consistent with it.

Along with the techniques of observing yourself outlined in the previous chapter, begin practicing observing your mind for any negative or doubtful thoughts you may have. Once you have gotten pretty good at noticing these thoughts, transform them into positive ones in that very moment.

Catch them and transform them, and do it as often as possible. For example when you find yourself saying, "I am stressed out!" take a moment along with a deep breath and say, "I feel pressure right now, but that is ok because I am smart, I am calm, and I can get through it." You may not believe it at first, but with consistency you will. Remember that it was the power of thought that got you to believe false things about yourself, so it will also be the power of thought that will help you to believe in yourself again.

Singular Meditation Exercise

Practicing the singular method of meditation helps affirm this technique of mind control. You can look in a book or online for a word, a sentence or couple of sentences that truly speak to you and use them for this technique, or you can come up with your own. Make sure that this phrase speaks to a quality that you hold in high regard and one that you resonate with. You will know it is the right one when you feel it. If you read it and it moves you to the point where you feel the urge to proclaim, "Yes! This feels so right!" then you have found it. Make sure it is one that is uplifting and positive for you without looking down upon others.

You can borrow Gandhi's quote, "I am the change I wish to see in the world," for example, or something as simple as, "Relax," or "I love myself," are good to use as well. Try your best to be aware of your personal defenses. You may think immediately, "Well yes, of course I love myself," but if this were true throughout, you would not have moments of doubt or insecurity. Be open to the practice and stay honest with yourself as much as possible. You will begin to break through your subconscious defenses and open yourself up to a vulnerable state where real significant changes may be allowed to happen.

Once you have chosen your phrase, find a nice quiet place to practice your mantra and turn off all distractions. If you are living in a busy household, tell the others that you do not wish to be disturbed for the next 15 minutes. Give yourself this amount of time to practice this meditation. If you are living in an apartment building with lots of noisy tenants, go outside and find a peaceful park or courtyard. You can also try to find a time where the environmental noise is at a low point during the day or evening.

Now begin focusing on your breath. Start at your normal rhythm and equalize the length of your inhale with your exhale. Once you have established this rhythm, deepen your breaths to a comfortable degree. When you are at a steady pace with your breathing, begin with an inhale and then on the exhale say your mantra out loud or to yourself. Focus on the feeling the word or phrase brings you and allow it to permeate every cell in your body. Continue saying your phrase on each exhale, focusing on the words as you say them and the feeling they bring you. Do this for the entire 15 minutes. It is as simple as that! It may feel silly at first, but the effects are amazing – in the moment, you will begin to notice how the power of these positive words actually do affect the feeling of your mind and your body. For example just saying the word, "Relax," slowly in this way truly begins to relax the muscles in your body where you hold tension such as your forehead, temples, back of the neck, shoulders, chest, and lower back.

You can always change your phrase as it suits you and experiment with different ones, but once you find one that really works you should stick with it for a while. By practicing this for 15 minutes on a daily basis, you will begin to dissolve those negative thoughts and replace them with the powerful belief of your phrase. It will permeate into your daily life as well. After a time, when you start to feel stressed or anxious in your daily life, you may have to actively tell yourself your phrase in that moment for a while, but eventually it will automatically kick in and help you to see the situation for what it really is without being overcome by those straining emotions.

Guided Meditation

When it comes to the practice of meditation, many people enjoy the guided method because it gives them something a bit more tangible to focus on and stimulates their imagination, whereas they may not have many other outlets to use their imagination elsewhere in their daily life. Guided meditations are done by listening to someone narrating and leading us through a sequence of particular things to think about with vivid imagery.

This method is designed to divert the logical side of brain function and thinking that follows strict sets of rules for problem solving which make finding a true solution difficult. It bypasses the clutter of thoughts we have that do not work for us and takes us deeper into our subconscious to better understand how our individual minds are working and where we may need to place focus on our way of going about things. There are also guided meditations that take us on a deep journey to the inner self where we may gain insights and understand ourselves better, perhaps even discover a trait or activity that we had forgotten about and would enjoy taking up again.

There are multitudes of guided meditations out there, designed for all different purposes. Take a quick search into

YouTube and you will see just how many there are. You can also find several on Amazon.com. Try a few out and see which ones you like. If you have a particular purpose in mind for doing the meditation, you will be likely to find something by searching for a guided meditation along with that specific topic. For example, "guided meditation for increasing self-awareness," or "guided meditation for boosting self-confidence," are a few that might help you find what you are looking for. Most of them are around 15 to 30 minutes long.

I would like to cover a few things about guided meditation that fall under stereotypes of the practice and while they can be funny, these kinds of opinions can dissuade people from the benefit of it. You may know what I am talking about, like that stereotypical long, drawn out voice that always seems to go with them. Why is that? They sound like they are trying to lull you to sleep! But actually, that is a part of it. If you remember your parents ever singing you a lullaby as a child or if you simply know the nature of lullabies then you get the idea.

The slow, singsong voice is meant to be soothing and relaxing while aiming to calm that busy mind of yours. Also, because meditations are working directly with the subconscious level, the mind needs to be brought to a deeper state than the one you are used to using throughout the day. This means that by using a soft intonated voice, you are more easily brought into a state of semi consciousness where the meditation is most effective.

Another thing that you will find stereotypical among guided meditations is their association with nature. Many meditations are always bringing you through a meadow or a forest or a garden of some such thing and you may find yourself thinking, "What is with all the greenery? I guess at least I don't have to worry about insects in these places!" Well, like it or not, as much as some people would like to consider us civilized and evolved beyond the grasses, we are still very much tied in with nature.

We need plant life to complete the gas exchange so that we can breathe the oxygen-rich air that nourishes our brains and cells. The phases of the moon directly affect our physiology and brain chemistry. And if you have read any literature, as I am sure you have, you know about the countless poets and novelists who are inspired by nature. There are entire magazines dedicated to gardening. It is a phenomenon that the more we connect with nature, the more we feel at peace. We have simply forgotten this.

Many guided meditations bring us back into this natural environment to touch upon that sense of peace and comfort along with the visual stimulation of vivid colors and organic life. In this way, they are getting us back in touch with that part of ourselves that we have forgotten on many levels, just as they are designed to help us get back in touch with the part of ourselves that is confident, creative, spontaneous, and knows what we like with the vitality to go after it, uninhibited!

Your Mind is a Garden

Although this is not a particular meditation, and there are many meditations out there designed for you to create your own vast garden, it will provide you with a further visualization and association of how the mind works and how different thoughts affect the mind to determine your overall sense of being.

As we have seen in children, the mind is an extremely fertile ground for ideas to be planted, take root, and to grow. It does not matter if these ideas are good or bad ones, the nature of the mind provides the environment for them to grow regardless. We can see that from discussion earlier in this book and life in general. In accordance with this association, good ideas are considered those that will beautify your mind and sense of being such is as flowers, shrubs and trees while bad ideas can be viewed as weeds. If you are familiar with the book *The Little Prince* you will see this same analogy described in the first few chapters. If you have not read the book, I recommend you take a look into it as it is very endearing and a short read. If you have read it, I recommend you reread it all the same.

For anyone that has had some experience gardening, they can tell you it takes work and a fair amount of maintenance. You need to make sure that your beautiful plants get the proper amount of sunlight and water, and it always provides benefits to talk to them in a caring manner. First of all this is because when you are talking to them, you are also exhaling carbon dioxide which helps them to grow. Second of all and more interestingly, extensive studies have been done on plants that are a bit controversial because they have concluded that plants are in fact sentient beings that respond well to positive encouragement and respond to negative stimuli by stopping growth or withering altogether. The other side of maintaining a garden involves catching weeds as soon as they appear and uprooting them before they grow. This is because, if neglected, weeds will run rampant throughout your garden congesting it and begin to choke the life out of your beautiful plants.

We can make a direct correlation to the ideas and thoughts that take root in our minds, and this is why garden meditations can be so effective. We must observe and maintain our thoughts with a nurturing attitude to ensure that they serve us well and help to promote our best intentions in living our lives, pursuing our dreams, and engaging in relationships on a daily basis. If we have good thoughts, we must see to it that they flourish by continuing to learn, developing ourselves, and reinforcing them with other positive thoughts.

In putting these positive thoughts to practice, we actively nourish them to take root where we can then see the fruits of our labor blossom over time and reap those fruits with the satisfying and sustaining relationships we have cultivated not just with other people, but with ourselves. Along with that, we may cultivate the garden of all the work we put into our lives to see projects come to fruition that will keep giving back to us as well as others, making this world a much more pleasant place to live.

In the same light, we must keep watch on our train of thought for negative thoughts – the weeds – and see to it that they are removed quickly. If we are not aware of these negative thoughts or pass them off as insignificant, they will most assuredly grow to the point that they become a problem and begin to infringe upon our behavior and daily activities. That is why you will see with further examples in abusive relationships later on in this book, if you allow one set of negative circumstances to invade your self-esteem, it will encroach into your other relationships without you noticing and over time you see other relationships beginning to deteriorate without understanding why it is happening. Take an active role in nurturing your mind and your inner self by learning how to identify your negative thoughts and remove them from your belief system before they drain other parts of your life. Treat yourself with care.

There was a very good book called "Eat, Pray, Love" by Elizabeth Gilbert and if you have trouble actually stilling the mind, this wouldn't be a bad choice of book because she experienced the same thing. She tried too hard. What she found that she was doing when asked to meditate was fighting within her mind the idea of thinking of nothing. People don't find this easy at all in the beginning stages of meditation.

Remember, you can make a whole load of difference to your life if you are able to meditate because it changes the pattern of thoughts. It allows you time to heal from all the negative things in your life and it means that you are able to move forward with a very positive and energized outlook. That's something that is lacking when you have self-esteem issues. Thus, meditation will help you and every moment that you are thinking about your breathing or a mantra during meditation, you are reducing the amount of negativity that you are subjecting your mind to, and that's positive input from you to your mind. That positive input helps to make you a much stronger person.

Chapter 12 – What Professionals Say About Self-esteem

If you think of self-esteem in terms of a curve drawn so that it rests upon a straight line, at one side of the curve, you will have low self –esteem. At the opposite side, you will have high self-esteem and at the top of the arch made by the semi-circle you will have normal self-esteem. It is a good idea to draw one of these semi circles and see where you believe your own self-esteem to be on the scale. You can judge this by your happiness level because at either end of the scale, you are unlikely to be a happy person. Both high and low self-esteem affect your personality and your emotional responses to life. Draw your scale and be as realistic as you can because, during the course of this book, it is intended that we help you to improve your rating.

The things that you are likely to experience if you have low self-esteem issues are that you look at the cup as half empty rather than half full. Let's look at some notable differences between people who have high self-esteem and those who have low self-esteem so that you get an accurate picture of where you are on the scale.

People with Low Self Esteem	People with High Self-Esteem
Underachieve through fear of failure	Overachieve to prove their worth
Believe themselves worthless	Believe themselves to be worth more than others
Believe that they cannot do things	Are overconfident that they can do things and take too much on
Believe themselves to be unacceptable in appearance	May be overly confident about the way they look
May believe that everyone else is more deserving	Believe themselves to be more deserving
Believe that others have more to offer	Believe that they have more to offer than others
Feels unloved	Feels overly confident in love but actually fails
Feels unwanted	Feels essential
Feels undeserving	Feels very deserving
Feels afraid to try new things	Will try new things no matter how capable they are.
Feels compared to others	Wants to be compared favorably to others

You can see from this table that these two character types are miles apart. Their expectations are unrealistic on both sides of the scale and the person who has high self-esteem is every bit as vulnerable as those with low self-esteem. They can burn themselves out by believing themselves to be invincible. They will not be well liked because of their need to compete all the time.

By now, you should have an idea about the scale of your problem and that is good because that means that you can work on the areas that affect you the most. Psychologists say that people who have self-esteem issues that are on the low side tend to be:

- More withdrawn
- Less likely to volunteer
- Socially inept
- Uncomfortable with people
- Uncomfortable with new situations
- They do not take risks
- They lack self-confidence

If you see yourself in any of these statements, do not be alarmed. Normal people have descriptions too from a psychological viewpoint but you need those descriptions to decide how serious your problem is, so that you can address it. You need to be extra honest with yourself because avoiding issues is what people with low self-esteem tend to do, and if you want to get beyond it, honesty is the only way.

Up until now, we have generalized about ways that you can improve your self-esteem but in the future chapters we are going to get more specific so that you can use the exercises shown to improve your weak points.

Exercise in self-assessment

What you can do is compare each of the elements in the table above with how you see life. Draw a parallel line and remember that above the line is too confident while below the line is not confident enough. Use each of the values in the table and measure how you approach life. If you do have self-esteem issues, chances are that most of your responses will be below the line.

You need to work toward being in the center somewhere – not too shy and not too over-confident. Try doing things to boost one of these and mark it down on your chart. I always tell people to start the chart with a red line and then mark changes with another color so that they can see improvements because often it's when you see improvements that you realize the significance of the changes that you make to your life.

Chapter 13 – Overcoming Fear of Failure

It is easy to see why someone with self-esteem issues would develop a fear of failure. One child at a school where I worked had this fear because his father threatened him with the slipper if he failed. Thus, his fear came from a real tangible fear of his father. Parents have a lot to answer for when it comes to children who have fears. Grown-ups who also have fears may have them left over from childhood or from making mistakes that took away their confidence. This is how many fears propagate throughout generations, and this is why I am very happy for you in choosing to read this book, and as well you should be happy and proud of yourself for choosing to work on yourself. By really taking this information and these suggestions throughout the book to heart, you are putting a stop to this generational cycle of fear in its tracks.

This should be a very exciting time for you because as you practice the various suggestions throughout this book and find your confidence improving, you will come to realize that everything begins with the self. The more that we focus on living to be our healthiest, happiest selves, the more that that positivity will resonate with the environment and the people in that environment around us. We generate an influence on others, and positivity and confidence are always more influential than negativity. Have you ever walked down the sidewalk or been in a public place where you noticed someone with a huge, genuine smile on their face and found yourself smiling as well? Or have you ever heard someone laughing so candidly, even if it sounded over-the-top, that you could not help but let out a giggle yourself? We are often influenced by children's reactions in this way because of the commonly assumed nature of their purity; that most everything that comes from children is genuine, uninhibited and refreshing.

The only reason this changes as we grow up is because we learn from our role models and society to fear things. We are taught to curb our enthusiasm instead of how to channel it into something productive. We are taught not to be so inquisitive because "Mommy or Daddy said so." We learn from our peers to conform in dress and behavior because "being different is weird, and that is bad."

The most sinister thing we are taught at a young age is to dream big and go after our dreams until we reach budding ages where we have the potential to start making those dreams happen, and then the tone changes and we are taught to be 'realistic' and 'get our head out of the clouds' because it is very rare for people to actually realize their dreams so we should 'save ourselves the disappointment'. That, or 'nobody has done that before,' or some other incriminating judgment, and while we may not believe them at first, it is still a seed that is planted in our minds. So if we do not work to rid our minds of that other person's belief, it will grow over time and we will end up settling for something less than what we truly wanted to go after and convince ourselves "oh, I was young when I wanted to do that," or in a mindset of self-doubt we tell ourselves, "I did not really want that anyways." By this example, we have ultimately allowed ourselves to give in to the negative beliefs of others, and the truth is they only say those things because they got sucked into the same way of thinking from the generations before them.

These basic fears and doubts begin to violate our sense of self-esteem which we develop coping mechanisms for, and many times just by the natural tendency to mimic the behavior of those whom we look up to, we take on their coping mechanisms without realizing it. These self-doubts and fears then transpose into other aspects of our lives without our realizing it.

Let's take a situation and show you how to turn it around. You fear taking your driving test for example. You are worried that you will not make it and that you will have to explain to friends and family that you failed. I know what this fear is like as it is one that I had to overcome. The first time that I took my driving test, I was very young and inexperienced. I told everyone I expected to pass and looked a complete fool when I failed. The next time that I took the test, I was a little older but I still had the leftover stigma attached to getting through the test. This time, I needed to pass the test in order to advance in my work and if I failed, there was more to lose than just pride.

I battled with the idea for the whole week before the test. Every time that I thought about the test, I made mistakes in my driving lessons until the teacher showed me a very clever trick. This can be applied to any situation in life.

Change your mindset

What this does is change your approach. He said that if I just thought of it as a comfortable half hour ride in the car, I change my mindset and I relax more because I am not seeing it as a test. It was a little difficult to do, but I thought that I had nothing to lose and went along with it. As it happens, it was the best advice in the world and I sailed through the test.

When your mindset tells you that there is a chance you will fail, you will continue to fear. If you change that mindset to a more casual approach, you also increase your chances of success, but do not depend on it. Instead, do not even think of whatever it is that you have to do as a test. Think of it as a normal activity on a normal day and think to yourself that you just have to follow the logical course of events. Chances are that fear will go away if you can manage to do this. Again, as with anything, to get better at it you must make it a consistent practice. The more that you practice this, the better you will get at it and you will begin noticing results within a surprisingly brief amount of time.

When you take the pressure of performance off of anything you do, you provide yourself more space to make accomplishments happen. Your mind becomes freer to get creative and relaxed with whatever it may be that you are engaged in because you have removed yourself from operating under stress, which is always constrictive to your efforts. Some of the more hardworking folks claim that they work well under stress and this is even seen as a positive trait in the working world because the demands to perform can be very stressful.

Stress could be considered as a motivator because it requires you to take things a bit more seriously, pay more attention, and increase your efforts at being more effective in your productivity. However this is only true for a short period of time. People who are constantly working in stressful environments begin to accumulate that stress in their minds and bodies on a subconscious level. They must develop coping mechanisms or their efforts will dwindle over time, and many of these coping mechanisms may seem temporarily helpful like drinking more coffee or energy shots, but they ultimately add to stressful states over time.

Instead, practice the idea of working well by being prepared and developing this healthy, relaxed mindset that we are discussing. Then you can say that you work well regardless of the environment because you have trained yourself to circumvent stress. You can make this a mantra to practice in helping change your mindset as well and you will find it very empowering. People around you will become impressed by your confidence and abilities and want to know what your secret is.

A good example of just how a person's change in mindset affects their state of being can be reflected in the following scientific study conducted some years ago. Some psychologists wanted to see just how much the mind has an effect on the body and a change in the psyche, or a person's sense of wellbeing. They conducted an experiment involving a group of maids at a hotel where they asked them questions about their routine away from work such as whether they exercised, what their diet was like, how much they weighed at the time and so on, all being health related. Then they asked the maids whether they considered the chores of their work to be exercise, such as changing the sheets, cleaning the bathrooms, vacuuming, etc. Most all of the maids did not consider their work to be exercise, they just thought of it as routine tasks.

The psychologists recorded all this data and then split the group into two. They allowed one group to go about their work and told them that they would check in on them in a month, asking them not to change anything about their routines or diets outside of work. Then they went to the second group and told them that all the tasks that they did at their work really are considered to be exercise, and they presented each of them with a sheet of information outlining the tasks and how many calories each burned. They told the second group of maids to keep this in mind while they were working and asked them just as the first group not to change anything else about their routines or diets outside of work. A month later, the psychologists checked back in with both groups of maids and asked them about their weight. Even though both groups performed the same kinds of tasks at the hotel, the psychologists found that the second group of maids, knowing that their work was actually engaging in exercise, had overall lost a significant amount of weight compared to the first group, whose overall weight remained the same as in the beginning of the month.

Do you see now how a person's mindset holds a great power over their sense of wellbeing? I will refer you back to the chapter of learning about your good points and practicing exercises in self-indulgence. The example of the maids goes to show that by being more aware of the activities that you participate in while engaging as much of your senses as possible, you are stimulating a change in your mindset to activate a greater sense of awareness, appreciation and gratitude for yourself, your actions, and your environment. This difference in mindset not only improves your perspective of the world to help you feel better about yourself and your situational circumstances, it alters your brain's and body's physiology to keep that change balanced, hence you really are creating a new you.

Measuring yourself against others

Let's have another look at things that you may fear about not being as good as other people. This is another feeling that can make you fear situations. If you have to do something in your life and you know that you will be compared with others, without self-esteem, you will fail unless you try a new approach. Try making your goals easier on yourself by knowing what you can do and just doing it. In this life, you do not have to measure up to others. It is only your perception. If you doubt your abilities in any area, say so. You can ask for help without being perceived as a failure. Bruce Lee, a man who was constantly involved in pushing his limits and breaking boundaries, has been quoted saying, "Fear comes from uncertainty; we can eliminate the fear within us when we know ourselves better." If you make it your job to know yourself, what is there to fear?

Change your goalposts:

I am doing this because I want to please the boss

That is not a good goalpost. You expect your boss's approval. Take that out of the picture and you also take out the worry about whether the work you do will please him or her. Do not do things to please others. Do the tasks because they give **you** pleasure. Change your mindset and do the work for **YOU**.

I am getting this done because it needs doing and I can do it

That is a much healthier approach because you are reinforcing that you can do the job. You are not concerned about other people's approval and you know the job needs doing. It is positive and there is no obligation to please anyone but yourself.

Fear of failure comes when you are trying to live up to other people's expectations. Their expectations are not your concern. They are their problem. Do what it is that you can do and enjoy doing it for yourself, not for their approval.

Exercise: Look into why you do things that do not please you and work out a way that you could do them and please yourself. That's vital because if you feel that you are always doing things to please others, there is no real pleasure for you and you need a share of pleasure in life as well as being helpful to others.

Chapter 14 – Gaining Confidence

The problem with people who have self-esteem issues is that they exaggerate things. They do not do this intentionally, but it is just their way of dealing with life. For example, what is the worst-case scenario if you do something wrong? You see it as humiliation and reinforcement of the fact that you are not good enough. It is nothing of the kind and that is your self-esteem issue talking. Today's failures become things that people laugh about tomorrow.

If you think that you are a failure at something, you need to start taking baby steps toward gaining confidence. The best way to gain confidence is to make sure you have your fair share of doing something that you know you are good at. Everyone has strong points and even people with self-esteem and confidence problems will have things that they excel at. The best way to find out what these jobs are is to sit with a piece of paper in front of you and write down the things that you enjoy doing. Usually people enjoy doing things because they are within their comfort levels. For example, I enjoy cooking and know I am good at it. Your likes may be totally different, but these are good starting points to gain confidence.

Your day should consist of a fair share of things that you are good at because these help you to build up your confidence. The reason this works is that if you are performing things you are comfortable with for 50 percent of the time, then that is 50 percent positive input for your confidence levels. Make sure that you choose things you enjoy doing that fit in easily with your lifestyle.

I can tell you that when I began writing articles for a publisher I was pulling my hair out, screaming in my room and shaking from anxiety for the first week. The work was very demanding with a high volume content to turn out in a short period of time. I was very poor at time management. I was familiar with the material I was writing about but I did not have a large enough knowledge base to meet the schedule demands fluidly. I had always dreaded deadlines ever since I was a little kid and avoided them at all costs, which affected my grades in college and my reputation in other jobs. I enjoyed the freedoms that the article job provided like allowing me to form my own schedule and choose what to write about to some extent, but under this much stress I felt incompetent in my capabilities and wanted to throw in the towel and quit at times out of blind fear of failure and frustration.

I really enjoy writing; I enjoyed the experience the job provided me in building a career as a writer along with the freedoms it provided. So instead of abandoning one of my passions by giving into my fear of failure and sense of self-defeat that was crushing my confidence, I decided to stick with it. I realized though that my attitude about deadlines and my approach to the job had to change. The turning point came when I took it upon myself to research more about the business I was getting involved in. I read up on other writers who were successful and the tips they offered. I started recording the times that I was actually working and the hours that I was taking breaks or getting distracted to help keep me on task, stay focused, and develop consistency. When it came to article topics that I did not know enough about, I gave myself ample time before hand to research as much as I could on the topic so that when it came time to writing, the information would be fresh and flow more fluidly.

All of these things were helpful and allowed me to gain more momentum at my practice. I regained some self-confidence, which was reassuring. However I noticed that I was still falling short of the mark when it came to those darn deadlines! I saw that even though I was making headway at being more effective in my work, I was still feeling stressed from just the idea of working under a deadline, and in that stressful state I would still procrastinate from doing my work. While I was at work, my thoughts about the article material would come slowly and my mind felt clouded because of the stress. All those subconscious memories of having failed before in school and other jobs were subtly plaguing my performance. My self-esteem took another hit and I began doubting myself again.

Luckily for my stubborn character, I was determined to see it through. I realized I had to change my mindset again, but in a much more frightening way this time – I had to confront my fear of failure that I had been living with and avoiding for such a long time directly. How did I do this? Well, one thing that helped was that I had been working on many of the exercises outlined in this book like meditation, positive affirmations, and negative thought observation and transformation for a number of years in other areas of my life. I had the right tools at my disposal and it was time to put them into practice for one of the biggest issues that was holding me back from living one of my dreams. I knew as well that by working at this issue in this particular area of my life, the resulting benefits would spill over into other areas of my life in which I felt held back. Just by knowing that, believe it with my whole heart, it made me feel better and boosted my confidence a bit.

I had to affirm to myself that I am not a failure. I looked in the mirror at myself or found a quiet spot where I told myself how much I love me because I am being courageous for going after my dream despite all the setbacks and failures. I said that I appreciated myself for taking this point in my life to turn myself around, and that I will succeed because I enjoy writing, I am good at it, and I will not stop trying. I did this for fifteen minutes at the beginning of each day when I would want to procrastinate from work the most and during breaks in between work. Whenever I felt the stress surmount while I was working, I took a short five minute break to do some breath work or a meditation exercise to clear my mind. I also changed my diet from excessive coffee and sweets to more fruits and vegetables that I knew would boost my energy levels in a much more positive way. I also cut out a two-hour morning routine to do some cardio exercise along with stretching and breathing work. I knew that this would promote better circulation and energize my body, providing a clearer mind and feeling of satisfaction that I was really doing well nurturing my body and mind. This morning routine really set my day off right and prepared my psyche for a really enjoyable, productive day.

Believe me, this did not happen overnight, far from it actually. I had to slide each practice into place little by little over about a month and once I developed somewhat of a consistency with them, it took another couple of months to hold it all together. I used my sense of stress as a gauge and a reminder to engage in one of these practices as I felt the onset of it. What kept me going if anything was knowing that it did not feel good being stressed out or giving up on doing something I loved. I was determined to feel good about myself. Really, who wouldn't be? So little by little, I was patient with myself and pushed myself a bit when I needed it, knowing that it was going to be a process and that it would pay out big over time.

By turning my focus on these positive practices, I had completely forgotten about deadlines altogether! And by sticking with these practices in little 10 to 15 minute slots here and there, my sense of stress dwindled and my productivity made leaps and bounds. I regained my confidence in a beautiful way, and when I looked back at all I had done, I could not stop smiling. I still wear that smile to this day, and sometimes I catch other people noticing me and a smile peeks out on their face too.

Remember that you do not have to rely solely on your own devices to make the change you wish to see in yourself. Let your friends and family members that you trust know about your intentions and ask them for their support. Ask them to check in with you from time to time to see how you are doing. You can even request that they help you stay on task when you feel like you need it. Your loved ones will surely be willing to be there for you. If you are unsure or are doubtful, watch out! That is a negative thought there and it only serves to hold you back. You never really know until you ask. You might as well try because you will have nothing to lose (and that is the attitude we are going for here that is so enabling

99

for people to accomplish goals), so speak up! You may be pleasantly surprised.

Getting more accomplished with tasks you are not comfortable with

Over the years, life has taken away your confidence. It did not happen overnight and you will not get quick results to help you to build them back up again. We have already talked about the way that you perceive things. Now, you need to look at the things that make you shy away from tasks or certain social situations.

- Meeting people

- Jobs given to you at work

- Getting things done on time

- Fear of new work practice

- Fear of speaking up

All of these may be on your list of things you do not feel confident doing, so let's take them one by one and the process that we use is one that you can apply to any situation. Each item needs to be broken down into easy tasks at first so that you regain your confidence and can learn to come out of your shell.

Meeting people

You may not be a social butterfly but you are not alone in this. There are many people who shy away from going out and meeting people. If you are shy of this very situation, think of the list of things that you wrote of things you enjoy and do well. You can use this as an introduction to like-minded people. For example, if you like photography, why not join a club. You instantly have people within your circle of new acquaintances that have a common interest with you. That always makes meeting new people a lot easier. Suppose you enjoy cooking. Why not invite people that you know and are comfortable with to come for a meal in your home? This could be family members or people that you know and trust. Friends and family who do not criticize you are the best ones to start with. This will give you more confidence about your socializing abilities and bit by bit, you can widen that circle until meeting new people is not a problem anymore.

If you are interested in meditation, a yoga class puts you in touch with people who are generally gentle in their lives. These are people seeking self-improvement just like you are and a yoga class gives you an opportunity to meet people in a friendly and welcoming situation. The equation that you need in order to overcome feeling inadequate with new people is:

Association – Associate that person with something you enjoy doing and you will not feel uncomfortable.

Find the interest first – Then introduce yourself to somewhere where like-minded people will congregate – Enjoy the interaction.

New relationships with strangers do present difficulty for people who have issues with self-esteem, but if you already have something in common, that makes it a lot easier for you to practice socializing and you can gradually widen the circle as you gain more confidence.

Being Comfortable Alone

Often people who have self-esteem issues are unable to enjoy even something as simple as being on their own. They may seek friendship so desperately that they make mistakes with the relationships that they do form. They see themselves as being incomplete. They certainly would never admit to self-love, and try to find the missing elements of their lives in unsatisfactory relationships. Someone who gets attached to another human being who is damaged can manipulate the situation and take control. While that may suit the individual with self-esteem issues in the short term, it is not going to be a healthy relationship to be in. If your partner sees you as weak and defective, eventually the relationship will falter. It can go one of two ways:

- He or she will not respect you and will add to your self-esteem issues

- He or she will manipulate you so that you are never in control of your own life

You need to gain confidence in who you are because until you do, you are not ready for a close relationship and may just be setting yourself up for more heartbreak. Strongmen who go for weak women will always take control and the relationship can end up as an abusive relationship. You should understand that these types of men (or women) are not actually strong either; by preying on weak people, they too have self-confidence issues that they are exerting on another. If your partner has to take the initiative in being strong all of the time, there comes a point when a relationship breaks down because relationships have to be a two-way street in equal proportions. If they are not, then there is a lack of respect and that can add to self-esteem issues. Look at these phrases:

- I need you

- I cannot live without you

The point is that any one human being is capable of being comfortable living on their own and you need to reach that point before you jump into a relationship so that you go into the relationship as a whole, rather than a needy partner. Otherwise, you are not offering all that you could be offering and that is not fair.

Your confidence in yourself is very important to deal with before jumping into a relationship. People who respect themselves do not give in to others who show disrespect. Likewise, people who respect themselves are more likely to receive respect from others because their personality automatically draws respect to them by magnetism. People who are complete without another person are able to go through life on their own terms and are less likely to be put down and insulted in the same way as people who have no self-esteem are.

How to build up your own self-confidence

Affirmations help with confidence levels. You need to put yourself into a situation where you are happy with what you are doing. Look at things that you know that you enjoy and make sure that the percentage of things you do that make you happy is larger than the percentage that causes you to doubt.

For example, I enjoyed writing poetry. It was not going to earn me a living, but it was something I did rather well. I kept a journal, and in that journal I placed my poetry. That was a morning exercise. I enjoyed music, so learned a musical instrument. That gave me a whole heap of confidence because when you play the piano, you imagine yourself as a concert pianist. When I play my guitar, I put all of my emotions into it and I know that even if the music is not perfectly played, I am improving. These are positive and enjoyable things that help me to gain confidence. I used to say, "I cannot do the F chord" on the guitar but it was only a question of persistence until I could. The more you practice things that you enjoy, the better you become at them.

There is a quote made famous by Albert Einstein that perhaps you should think about putting to practice. The quote goes, "Practice anything for ten minutes a day and in a year's time you will have mastered it." A year may seem like a long way down the road but ten minutes a day for anything is time that any person can afford. So choose whatever skill you would like to master and put the deserved amount of time in for it. With all the other things going on in your life, by the end of a year you will be able to look back and amaze yourself with how much you have accomplished. Plus you will have a new talent to add to your repertoire, further enriching your life to the way you want to live it.

I have never used affirmations but I suppose in my own way, I do use positive statements that others may see as affirmations. When I want to achieve something, instead of saying it is difficult or giving up before I start, I tell myself "I can do this." Other people use this as a mantra when they look in the mirror and find that it gives them strength to achieve. Do what works for you, because something definitely will. If you keep on trying to find those things that you really enjoy doing, you will eventually be able to center your life upon them. For example, I was great at reading. I love books and found that I could use this skill to read to kids in the local library. It helped to take me out of my shell and spend time doing something that I respected and knew I was good at.

There was a time when I was unable to read heavy literature but I persevered. If you have things that are hard to do within your life, try altering the time that you do them. Hard work tasks are better done in the morning when you have energy. Hard reading is best done in silence. The reason you may be failing to reach your potential is because you let life get in the way. My meditation helped as well because it made my more focused on succeeding in my life and instead of thinking negative thoughts. I found myself discovering more and more enjoyment from doing things that I loved and fitting them into my otherwise busy life. The ideal is if you can find a job that you love, do it, even if it pays a little less, because the dividend that you get is that you are not so stressed and feel so much more capable. I excel at my job because it is a job that goes along with my personality and my temperament. The job fits me like a glove.

You need to look at your core values. Know what they are. Most people who have low self-esteem think better of others than they do of themselves. Caring professions are good environments for seeing your own true colors. They also help you to put things into perspective. Make yourself feel good about you by volunteering sometimes to give food to the homeless or to help friends that have kids. The positivity that comes from doing things like this makes life very worthwhile and in the meantime, you begin to gain confidence and see that you have value. Remember that by staying mindful while you engage in these activities and maintaining a positive attitude as often as you can, you will enrich your experience as well as your self-esteem.

All of your life, you have lived with your body and your mind. It is time to become comfortable with who you are. Try to trace the roots of why you feel bad about yourself. Write them down so you can read them back. They may appear as things like:

- My mother says I am stupid

- My father does not approve of my choices

- My sister is prettier than me

- My boss thinks I am an idiot

The reason that self-esteem issues enter into your life is because you let them. It is not what people say. It is the fact that you held on to what they said and allowed them to affect your own sense of self-worth. You need to learn that you are not defined by what other people say, no matter what age – from a little toddler to a grown adult. Now, what you have to do to regain confidence in yourself is to cross out each of the items on your list, and write something next to it:

- My mother says I am stupid - she does not always get everything right

- My father does not approve of my choices – These are my choices not his

- My sister is prettier than me – Yes, but prettiness does not define who you are

- My boss thinks I am an idiot – Then he needs to learn respect me

You allow yourself to be influenced by what other people say or think about you and that is why you have self-esteem issues. Every time you think of a negative situation in your life that fills you with dread, write it down and hen counterclaim it. Do not be defined by what other people think of you. I used to seek approval of my mother and never ever got it. I thought, as her child, I was entitled to it but instead of praising me for the good things that I did, she ignored those and pointed to the bad things. For many years, I let this become who I was. I was the bad person that my mother had decided I was and hid within that shell for years. The point is that you are NOT what people define you to be. You are an independent human being. When I realized this at quite a late age, I felt suddenly free. I did not need my mother's approval anymore and found that as long as what I did made me happy, and then the happiness that followed was lasting.

Before she died, she was totally miserable with who she was. I decided that when you try to own other people's lives and fail, it makes you very unhappy indeed. When I took ownership of my own life, just as she should have taken ownership of hers, I was able to succeed and be appreciated by people around me that did not have this preconception that I was a failure. If you surround yourself with other people's negative attitude of you, and count it as being important, you lose something of yourself. Listen to opinion, weigh up which opinion is helpful to you and which is not, but do not let it change your fundamental personality.

If you were to hear someone say cats are blue, you would not suddenly start believing that they were. However, for the past years, you have accepted statements which are equally ludicrous about who you are and have let them rule your life. It is time to let go and learn that any comment made to you is as ludicrous as the statement that cats are blue until you decide it has credence. If someone says, "You are hopeless," ask yourself – am I hopeless? If you are a positive person, you can dismiss a statement like that, or you can accept that in certain areas of your life you are hopeless. It does not make you less of a person. A brain surgeon may not be very good at house painting. Does that make him less of a person? Of course not, even though a friend may say to him when he dons the paintbrush "you are hopeless." The statement doesn't make him less of a person. It is just a fact that he is hopeless at painting and he would probably be the first to admit it. You don't have to be good at everything. There is no rule on earth that says you do. Be as comfortable with your failures as you are with your successes because they are all part of who you are.

In fact, use your failures to light up the way to success. Don't be afraid to admit that you approached something in the wrong way, but learn from it to do things in another way that works better. It's all about developing your skills and as you do, you will gain more confidence in yourself and be more in control of any given situation.

Chapter 15 – The Mistakes That People Make In Life

I remember a friend of mine having a garden for the first time in her life. Her husband had left her and she was living in a new home on her own and decided that she wanted to make the garden look nice. She had no experience and her ex tried to put her down in an argument one day. He said that she would make a mess of her garden like she did with everything else. We were all sitting outside drinking coffee when he made this statement. She had been tearful during the divorce procedure and she had lost a whole heap of self-confidence, as one does when faced with the fact that a loved one has chosen to leave them for someone else. I thought that her reply was very brave and very relevant and it may help you as much as it helped me to get things into perspective.

"God lets me make mistakes," she retorted, and there was not much more that he could say to make her feel bad about herself because she had realized that what she said was actually true. In life, regardless of whether you are religious or not, you are allowed to make mistakes. We all do it. I remember stuffing a duck with orange sauce instead of merely serving it up with it. Of course, I made a mess of the whole oven in the process, but when you look back on the mistakes that you make, you can actually find a very ironic and amusing side to them in retrospect.

The TV shows that show clips of people doing foolish things make audiences laugh is another example of the amusing mistakes that people make. Although the mistake may not seem very funny at the time it happens, retrospect makes it funny. People make mistakes and learn from them, but people will self-esteem issues do all kinds of mental gymnastics with their mistakes, and that in itself is the biggest mistake anyone can make. Look at these reactions to mistakes and learn from them, because you do not have to have a huge post-mortem every time you do something wrong. It is just a way of life and you need to brush off your hands and start again. It really does not matter in the slightest.

Results of Making Mistakes

Reaction of someone with self-esteem issues	Reaction of someone with no self-esteem issues
Everyone is looking at me	Gets up and takes a bow
Is scared to try that same thing again	Adjusts the approach and succeeds
Goes into his or her shell and gives up trying	Celebrates the success or gives up as a complete failure

Does not see failure as being acceptable	Accepts that failure is part of life
Uses that failure to reinforce negative self-image	Moves on and tries something else

The difference in the way that people see mistakes is astounding. You do not have to be perfect. There is no hard and fast rule that says you cannot make mistakes. The lady who stood up on stage with her skirt tucked into her panties didn't know that she had so much on display, but she saw the funny side of it in retrospect, whereas those with self-esteem issues would immediately add it to their list of sins and make themselves even more negative than they already are.

Perfection

No one on earth expects you to be perfect, except you. Give yourself a break and realize it is okay to make mistakes. Mistakes are what show that you are human. Do you remember seeing Meryl Streep playing the part of the fashion icon in the movie Prada? She expected everyone around her to act in a set way and everything had to be perfect. It is neither realistic nor is it possible for people to live their lives in this way. Drop the attitude that you fail if you do not get everything perfect. Human beings make mistakes, but they are allowed to. Some make classic blunders that are flouted across the media, but it does not make them less of a person than they were before the media got hold of the story. It just means that they had a bad day.

It is vital to look at the expectations that you place on yourself and that you also learn to laugh at yourself instead of criticizing. The mistakes we make are actually quite funny, although not at the time. Distance yourself from the mistake, look back on it and instead of seeing all the negative connotations, look for the humor. It is there if you look deep enough and it will help you to change your attitude about the mistakes that you make. You are not perfect. No one is. Do not try to be.

Exercise – Look at the table above and write down something that you believe you did wrong during the day. Then look at the healthy response to doing something wrong and adopt it. Try to change the way that you look at your mistakes. It makes a difference to the outcome if you can look at mistakes positively and move on with a positive attitude, rather than putting yourself down all the time and adding to the negativity in your life.

Chapter 16 – Overcoming Anxiety

Before you can tackle this, you need to know what situations cause you to feel anxious. Try to pinpoint them. You cannot do much about the situation if you do not know the trigger points, and making a list of these will help you. To try and assist you, the way to find these trigger points is to look back on the times when you were at your most anxious and try to determine what made you panic or what you made you feel uncomfortable.

Let's look at a whole host of potential triggers for nervousness or anxiety:

- He or she spoke to me and I was super nervous
- I was nervous when expected to do something I did not know how to do
- I was nervous when I sat down at the exam table
- I was nervous when his mother came to visit
- I was nervous when we went to a formal dinner

- I was nervous being at a party where I knew no one

These are all everyday situations that can bring on anxiety but it is not the actual situation that made you nervous. These are triggers. If you squeeze the trigger on a gun, the gunfires and all hell breaks loose. When you decide to react to one of these triggers, you pull that trigger and your problems start.

He or she spoke to me and I was super nervous

When someone that speaks to you makes you nervous, you need to react slowly. People who are nervous show this by blurting out the things that they want to say and can feel very foolish indeed, but they are not seen like that. By stepping back a little and taking time with responses, you enable yourself to regain your composure. Here, this would be an ideal time to use your breathing exercises. Breathe in deeply through the nose, be aware of the breath and breathe out. After you have done this, you have actually calmed yourself down so that you are in a better position to answer the question.

I was nervous when expected to do something I didn't know how to do

Everyone feels this inadequacy when asked to do something for the first time. The difference is that you actually expect yourself to be able to do it. The perfectionist part of people with self-esteem issues will tell them they have to succeed. They line themselves up for failure every time by expecting this. The best way around this trigger is to admit that you do not know how to do something, but that you are willing to give it a good shot. Never be afraid to ask for help. Not only does this take the panic away, but also you may actually learn to be a better person and a more capable person by depending upon someone who can show you how something is done. It makes them feel good too so you win allies along the way. If they move too quickly for you, ask if it is possible to explain in a simpler way. People requiring assistance offends no one. They do, however, get offended by people who give the impression they can do something and then fail through their own stubborn unwillingness to ask for help.

I was nervous when I sat down at the exam table

Believe or not, most people that sit at exams are nervous. If they are overly confident, chances are that they will fail because they take for granted their own superiority and these are the people who are on the other end of the scale of self-esteem. They think too highly of their own abilities. It is natural to feel nervous, but you can limit this a little. Get a good night's sleep before the exam. Tell yourself that fail or pass, you are still the same human being. That is vital. The only thing that hits your self-esteem levels is the way that you react to situations. So what if you fail? Does it really matter? If you think that it does matter, then your approach to exams needs to change. When people are anxious they deprive themselves of oxygen. When they do that, they panic more. It increases the heart rate. It increases the blood pressure and the anxiety becomes panic.

Before an exam, sit somewhere peaceful and breathe. If you get a moment for meditation, this is helpful and even a walking meditation can help you if you are in a situation where you cannot actually sit down or find that peaceful place to reflect. Walking meditation consists of concentrating on your breathing and counting the breaths while walking – perhaps in the college grounds or alongside a river or somewhere inspirational. This energizes the brain and helps you to face the exam room without it becoming a panic.

I was nervous when his mother came to visit

Let's analyze this situation. The mother-in-law or the potential mother-in-law is the cause of much stress. The man you love or that you care about is pre-owned by her. She has to let go of her little boy if you want to form a great relationship and some mothers-in-law just do not let go. It is not actually your fault and often people with damaged self-esteem levels measure themselves by how their mother-in-law measures them. This is a huge mistake and also one that may cost you the relationship between her and you. What she thinks does not matter in the least, but it does influence how positive your relationship is and that is why you worry. Talk to your loved one about this and let him/her be aware of your fear. This helps because if your loved one knows you are nervous, he or she will not put you in a situation that is difficult and is likely to make the future mother-in-law back off.

Remember that what she thinks of you is one thing. What your partner thinks of you is entirely different. If your partner loves you as you are, be yourself when you meet her. If that means making mistakes occasionally, she may actually find that endearing rather than seeing you as being incompetent. When you put on airs and graces to try and please someone else, you also put up barriers so that they never really see the real you. Of course, you should dress nicely out of respect for her. Of course, you should be polite and respectful. But you do not have to be someone you are not.

I was nervous when we went for a formal dinner

There are several reasons why nervousness would occur in a situation such as this. Again, it just needs a simple analysis and you will see there is no reason to be nervous. One reason that may cause your nervousness is not knowing how you measure up against other guests. As long as you check the kind of attire that people are expected to wear, you cannot go wrong on that score. For example, if you wore formal clothing, then you would be correctly dressed for the occasion. The problem is that people with self-esteem issues are perfectionists when it comes to looking inwardly. They expect themselves not only to be superman or woman, but also to be perfect. You are not and you never can be so why set yourself up for failure?

You may be nervous about the conversation you have to have with people that you do not know. Again, you are expecting too much of yourself. Small talk and politeness are simple rules to follow and you already know how to do that. Perhaps you are nervous about etiquette and what all those knives and forks are for. It is a silly fear, because all you have to do is follow the example of people around you and you will not make an idiot of yourself. Practice your observational skills.

You were nervous about going to a party where you knew no one

Logically, if no one knows you, no one has any expectation of you. The perfectionist in you wants to make an impression but does not know how to because there is no way of knowing whom these people are and what impresses them. You are doing it again. Let go of what other people think. It is not about them. It is about you.

If you do not want to attend a party where you know no one, then politely decline and stop the stress in its tracks. If you do want to go, but are nervous about the impression you have on others, think of it like walking down the street on an average day. Do you care about what the people that pass you think? Of course not. They are not part of your life. Thus, think of all these new faces at the party as strangers on the street. Their opinions do not matter until you get to know them and then they only matter to you if you become friends and find mutual respect for each other. And in the end, they still do not matter because as long as you know that you are trying to do the best for yourself and be the best person that you can be, no other person's opinions matter. Stop trying to please people or to make an impression. Just be yourself. The impression will happen naturally with ease.

The problem with people who have self-esteem issues is that they overthink everything and analyze situations, making them more complex than they need to be. Let's show you a ridiculous conversation to demonstrate what people with self-esteem issues do. It is unrelated but it demonstrates the pointlessness of analyzing:

Boy to girlfriend: Would you like to ride on the back of my motorcycle?

Girl thinks: Will people be able to see up my skirt?

Will it mess up my hair?

What if I fall off?

What if he is not much good at driving a motorcycle?

What can I use as an excuse without putting him off?

It is ridiculous. This amount of analyzing is silly because the situation does not call for it, and most of the time the things that worry people who have self-esteem issues don't matter. They make mountains out of molehills and avoid risk taking. They also look from every angle because they are so afraid of making mistakes. As you learned in the last chapter, you are allowed to make mistakes.

Being spontaneous – an exercise
The next time someone asks you to do something, just do it without analyzing it. It may be something as simple as passing something across the table or as complex as asking you to drive and pick them up in a place you are unfamiliar with. Say yes. Be spontaneous. Whatever it is, and as long as it is something you want to do, do it without thinking about all of the potential case scenarios. Get more proactive and

learn to gain confidence in your ability to make good snap decisions.

Do you want to come to the movies?

Yes, sure, what's on?

Instead of: Do I have something to wear? Will he try to kiss me in the dark? Will I know how to respond? Will the movie be good? Will we be able to find a parking space?

Stop torturing yourself and be spontaneous. The sooner you learn to use your initiative, the better. People with low self-esteem do not trust their initiative and do not use it sufficiently because of that lack of trust. Practice in front of a mirror. Hold two cards of different colors up in front of you. You need to prepare about a dozen of these. They can be colors, shapes, sizes but each must be distinctly different from its pair. Hold up the cards and make an instant decision.

Blue or white?   Answer without even thinking

Square or triangle?   Answer without thinking

Keep on doing this over and over again. What you are telling your subconscious is that your initiative needs practice and you need to be instant with your answers. This is a great exercise for self-assertion. Keep the cards. Add to them and practice daily because this hones your skills in decisiveness and being decisive is something people with self-esteem issues are not. Thus, the more you can give yourself this test with different cards to keep the game spontaneous, the more capable you will become at using your initiative to tell you the right answer when someone asks you a question.

Practicing this activity also helps you to learn more about yourself by recognizing which direction your snap decisions point to. It trains you to understand the nature of your own mind, your personal intuitive preferences and your personality at large. Get creative with the symbols that you put on the cards and have fun with it.

It will help you to learn more about where you should direct your efforts in life and lead to further opportunities to explore passions you may have not been aware of. Remember that repetition helps. If you have self-esteem issues, these didn't happen overnight. They happened over a period of time where reinforcement was negative. Now, you need to learn to trust yourself a little more and this exercise will help you to do that.

Chapter 17 – Learning To Trust Others

One of the greatest issues that people with low self-esteem have is that they either trust people who are untrustworthy and follow set patterns within their lives or they fail to trust anyone because they are afraid to let people into that safe little bubble in which they live. I had to point out the distinction because it is very relevant. If you do not think much of yourself, you settle for less than you are entitled to and many relationships are formed on an unequal footing because those with low self-esteem allow themselves to become less important in a relationship.

Typical examples can be given here of those who marry an abusive partner. Even if they eventually part ways, the chances are that the low self-esteem will then push them into another relationship, which is equally abusive. Why? The basic reason is because those who do not think that they deserve more than they have do not get it. There is a very wise and profound author named Don Miguel Ruiz whose books carry messages about this principle that can be read multiple times and each time the reader will gain further insights about them. He also has a knack for wording these bits of wisdom in a simple way so they can be easily understood at first glance. One of these bits of wisdom is that we allow others to abuse and control us as far as we respect ourselves, or rather, as far as we are lacking in self-respect. Once we have been pushed to that point we do not tolerate the abuse anymore and remove ourselves from it or remove the problematic person from our lives. For example, "He beats me because I deserve it." Unfortunately, those who believe a statement like that are likely to be with a partner that reinforces the low opinion of the subject being abused. These are typical statements that an abused person may hear:

- It was your fault. You could not stop, could you?

- You made me do this

- You do not appreciate all I do for you

Wake up. This kind of manipulation will worsen your opinion of yourself. People who abuse actually repeat over and over the same messages so that they become a part of day-to-day life for those they abuse. Just like the parent telling the child over and over that the child is no good, the abuser uses emotional blackmail to keep a partner in check and it is cruel and takes advantage of weakness. The problem is that when the abused went into the relationship, perhaps they went in thinking that the relationship would mend them. It does not work like that. You need to be whole when you get into a relationship so that you are able to work through problems without this kind of abuse. This is so important to remember. If you feel that you cannot live without having a lover or partner, you are not ready for a relationship. You need to already be whole. That is the mistake that the abused make over and over again because they cannot see how they can live a life on their own without a partner as a crutch. When the partner gets fed up of being that crutch, he/she pulls out the crutch and insults their partner so that they end up even more broken than they were when they started the relationship.

If you have found yourself in such a situation in the past or currently, something to help you understand the situation that will lend to help you feeling better with time is that abusers are also operating on self-esteem issues and they are not ready for relationships either. Their need to control or manipulate others is a projection of their own inadequacy to control and take responsibility for their own actions When you come into this understanding it will give the power they held over you back to you and help you to regain your confidence.

So how can you Trust People Again?

It begins with being able to trust yourself with the decisions you make. This comes along with the development of self-confidence and learning to be comfortable being by yourself. Make a practice of noting the actions that make you feel comfortable and the ones that do not, and this will help you to develop a healthy intuition in recognizing those people that truly make you feel comfortable and those that give you a valid reason to be uneasy or on guard around them.

You can assess your friendships to see which friendships give and take in equal proportions. Make a list of the people that you trust and ask yourself why you trust them. You will probably find that family members who are close and who have not caused you hardship make the top of the list. Then, there will be friends that have been in your life for as long as you can remember.

The people that you choose for this list must be people that you are completely comfortable with. This is the support team for your life. Friendships are valuable because they help to make us feel wanted and needed and the problem when you have low self-esteem may be that you are looking for friendship in all the wrong places. If, for example, someone you call a friend is always making you feel bad, then that is not truly the kind of friend that has a positive influence. You need to assess these things to establish which friends are the ones that you trust.

Feeling wanted and needed is fine, but seeing this as the purpose of friendships is what actually lends to looking in the wrong places. Without want, without need, you make yourself available to any and everybody, and then you can truly give your whole self without reservation, and without worrying about the balance of "who is doing what for me" that makes the relationship feel important. It comes with the notion of self-respect and an inner sense of security. It comes with the sense of being comfortable alone as we have discussed in the chapter earlier. With the inner strength of these principles, you can see friendships as those relationships where you simply enjoy each other's company and are able to share yourselves with each other more openly.

- Does the friendship add value to your life?

- Do you give and take on a regular basis?

- Would you trust this friend with your secrets?

- Does this friendship make me feel good?

If you can answer three out of four of these questions about a particular person, then they have hit the trust list. What circumstances did you meet under? Where can you find more friends of this kind of reliability? In an earlier chapter, I encouraged you to find an interest and find a friend by having something in common with people when you let them into your life. Now, you have to step further than that and find trust. Trust involves several things:

- Mutual respect

- Mutual interests

- Mutual feelings for each other

- Mutual sense of communication – this one can be a secure sense of verbal or written message exchange that does not leave you guessing what the other person means. It also refers to a certain silent understanding, where if you do not talk with the other person for a long while, it does not change anything in your relationship. You will both be able to pick up your connection right where you left off from the last time you talked.

If you can relate to someone through things that you are interested in, you will have already achieved one of these aspects of where trust comes from. Having mutual interests, feelings and respect makes for a very healthy relationship. It is worthwhile sometimes to go through your mental list of old friends and acquaintances because oftentimes we do not give people the respect that they merit and you may want to revisit some of these relationships and give them another try.

Making new friends helps to boost your confidence and it means that your support system is stronger. If you find people who respect you for your beliefs, for who you are or for the way you live your life, these are people that will help you to build up your self-esteem. They are positive, encouraging, friendly people and understand that empathy helps relationships rather than criticism.

There is also something to be said about true friends that will not just sugar coat their opinions all the time and be honest with you about their true notions. A real friend should be able to tell you how they really feel or their true opinions of your actions or words while still being sensitive and respectful of you. Do not write these types of friends off if you feel offended simply because they do not agree with everything you do or say. These people are valuable and will help you to grow further, being respectful while getting you to look at things that perhaps you are reluctant or unable to see for yourself.

Remember there is a difference between criticism and constructive criticism, so if you have trouble telling the difference then learn how to decipher between the two. Criticism will just leave you feeling bad with nothing to gain from it. Constructive criticism may make you feel uncomfortable at first, but it will give you something to think about and upon contemplation, will leave you with an open decision to adopt what was said that will help you to change for the better, or discard what was said with no hard feelings to the person who said it.

It took me a while to learn who was friend and who was foe but when I did, it made an absolutely amazing difference to

127

my life because I eliminated those people who added no value to my life. It was amazing how quickly I was able to see the difference to my life. Without negative influences, people were more respectful, they did not mind that I was not perfect and they knew what give and take was all about. That instantly boosted my life.

I no longer mixed with those who were long-term negative influences because I could not trust them to have my wellbeing at heart. They had proven to be the type of people who took pleasure at other people's misfortune and that was not the kind of friend I wanted to be associated with.

Breaking off ties with people like this is very easy. Make yourself unavailable. Make yourself busy with positive endeavors and you will find that they will go elsewhere and spread their misery somewhere else. Or you can exercise your newfound self-confidence by speaking directly to these people, telling them why you cannot be around them anymore. If they start to protest or make a case about it, be firm and simply tell them that that is the decision you have made for yourself, and then stick to it and follow through. This will help you feel better about being more assertive with yourself, with your relationships, and it will bring closure to those areas of your life that have brought you pain. It will also earn you respect, if not just for yourself, because you were able to confront the source of your issue directly, and that takes guts.

Feel empathy to a certain extent although you cannot have them in your life any more. These are people whose insecurities make them criticize others. They will not change until they are ready to change and if they ever do, you can welcome them back into your life as positive influences rather than the negative influences that they are now.

It takes a while to learn trust but as you add new friendships to your life, you are doing just that. You are showing that you have sufficient confidence to be able to invite others to become part of your friendship circle. You are also sending a clear message to negative influences that your life is too precious to waste on something that is negative.

Chapter 18 – Seeking Help in Understanding

In this book, I have tried to make everything as easy as possible for people to understand. If you fail to understand why you have issues with self-esteem even after flipping through the pages of this book several times, then perhaps you need to find professional help of some kind. A true friend can help by giving you answers to your questions about yourself and the way that you are with others, but a professional is detached from your life and you are therefore much more likely to be able to discuss openly with them the shortcomings you feel that you have in your life.

These may be coaches who can help with the question of confidence. They may be professionals who deal with such as things as phobias, which result in anxiety, or you could simply choose a psychologist who really does understand the dynamics of relationships and can explain it to you in a way that you totally get. It is important that you do understand why self-esteem issues are happening. If you do not, how can you put it right? There are specialists who deal with phobias, if these are bugging your life, and they will need to use their expertize to help you overcome those difficulties that put you into an anxious state, such as fear of flying, fear of spiders, etc. These are very specialized anxieties that require that a certain kind of professional input.

In the case of wanting to be more assertive, you can always go to self-assertion classes and you may just make some very good friends along the way that are experiencing the same problems as you and are unable to express themselves. Believe it or not, acting classes can also help because when you take on the roles of the characters that you play, you learn a lot about how different behavior affects the responses that you get in life. This also helps you to understand and adjust your own responses to problems that present themselves.

Another area where professional help is useful is in taking up meditation or yoga because both of these are disciplines that help you to find the calm within yourself that also makes you stronger and more able to face the world on equal terms. Sometimes, joining groups like these also mean that you get to see all different kinds of perspectives and will be able to really relate to people who learn with you.

Your self-esteem issues may be stunting your career. Why not seek the help of a psychologist or someone who coaches people to succeed? Some of these professionals are referred to with the title 'Life Coach.' These positive people reinforce the value of positivity and can really help you get back on track with your career which, at the same time, will help you in your general relationships within life. You may be failing because you expect to fail. You may be failing because you do not know how to succeed. All of these professionals have answers that can help with confidence levels, anxiety levels and also at showing you how to fix problems that may arise because of self-esteem issues.

In today's world, where it is a recognized thing that stress affects so many people, a large percentage of those who are affected by stress will have self-esteem related issues. That is over 350 million in just the United States. Your problem is not as rare as you may believe it to be. People you pass every day on the street or on the way to work may be suffering the same thing. The reason? Life is speeded up today. People are expected to achieve high levels of performance and not everyone can keep up with it.

Society has changed a great deal since the end of the last World War and women in the workplace is a common occurrence, but is that really an improvement? You may need both earning wages in a relationship in order to break even, but the stress that puts on your relationship with others and your ability to cope may be affected. You need to assess your life and find out where all of the negative input is coming from and a professional will be able to do this and mirror back to you what changes you need to make to make life a better place to live.

Countries in the world where there is not enough food or housing provide a really negative environment to their people in the way of material things. However, when you talk to people in the undeveloped world about their logical thought processes, what you do not find is people looking for solutions through medication. They do not have the money for medication. I was surprised in Africa when I encountered people in dire circumstances who were probably some of the most well adjusted people I have ever met. Why? The expectations of societies such as this are less. Parents are happy to encourage children to take up basic education. They are happy when a child achieves a very small achievement in comparison with the western world because the fact that the child is alive is what matters when you come down to it. In those circumstances, children who survive are positive statements about parental care and about changes for the better, so even if a child makes a mistake, he isn't labeled as he would be in the western world with labels that give the child self-esteem issues in later life.

It is a simpler society and one that the western world could learn a lot from. Professionals will be there to help you to learn new priorities that make your life a much more positive place to be and you can also help yourself considerably by looking at options that make your life more positive including all of those included within this book. Being an independent person, I sought the answers to my problems myself, but I have to admit that all of the lessons that I have learned over the period of my life have been valuable reinforcement of the fact that I have value. I also learned that I am entitled to an opinion and just because I have one does not make it correct. Also, I am allowed to make as many mistakes as it takes me to learn how things work to make my life a richer experience.

Earlier in the book, I talked about a friend whose husband had deserted her. She started out with a new house and a new garden and decided that she was able to make mistakes and that she would learn by them. Pulling up a valuable plant thinking that it was a weed, I remember her replanting it a couple of days later and apologizing to the plant. That plant now stands in proud testament to the fact that she is allowed to make mistakes, but that she was not too proud to do something once she had made the mistake. You will make mistakes along the way, and you have already done so, if you think that your worth is less than that of someone else. Life has thrown you all kinds of curve balls that send different messages. If you take the time to sit down and work out why, perhaps you can address a lot of the problems yourself, but you need to know that there are professionals available to help and guide you on your journey into finding out who you are and liking what you see. When you do, life starts to be a much more satisfying place to find happiness and contentment.

Who you are is not made up of other people's opinions of who you are. When self-esteem issues kick in, you pass responsibility to someone for your unhappiness and often take the blame yourself. You are not wrong. The people who criticize you are also not wrong. What is wrong is the way you receive criticism and what you do after it has been given to you. Assess its value, thank the critique, and move on with your life because if you take their criticism further than that, you allow it to eat into who you are and it is then that problems start to arise in your life and make your life a place that you actually hide from because you don't see yourself as worthy. That's nonsense. Of course you are worthy. You just need to understand that sometimes, people who criticize and try to make you feel small are smaller than you and do it to distract their attention from looking inwardly.

"Never be bullied into silence. Never allow yourself to be made a victim. Accept no one's definition of your life; define yourself." ~ Harvey Fierstein

Chapter 19 – Taking Baby Steps alone

If you have asked for help from a professional, there will come a time when you have to move on and live your life. The professional is there to guide you, but there will come a time when you have to look at your life and see where you are allowing negative influences to affect it. I used to think that negative thoughts were self-protection. If I was ready for the worst to happen and it didn't, the result was more positive. However, having reassessed this, what it meant is that I spend most of time thinking negatively, expecting the worst to happen and was not therefore very happy with my life.

Since changing my attitude, I have found that life does present some disappointments but not as much as when I was always thinking negatively. If I miss a bus, it's not a huge deal and the world will not fall apart. I used to think that I was so stupid that it was inevitable that at some stage I would miss a bus. What I hadn't realized was that I was always putting myself down as stupid and that's really not helping self-esteem at all. If you make your core being much stronger and filled with positivity, when you do miss the bus, it isn't a big deal at all and you don't blame your own stupidity like I did in the past. A few phone calls of explanation and the situation improves. It's a practical thing that went wrong and that happens all the time.

Try to imagine life as a river. You can either see it as being filled with stepping stones to help you to get through or being filled with crocodiles that will potentially bite you. It is far better to think of the stepping stones and take them one at a time. If you occasionally slip, it's not a big deal and the crocodile won't get you. You simply stand up, shake yourself off and get back up again, looking out for the next stepping stone and learning that perhaps you have the wrong shoes on or that you didn't look where you were stepping.

Prefer to look at opportunity – rather than disaster. If you go through life thinking of the worst case scenario, you build this up in your mind so much that you actually make the bad things happen. "I will fall over" would result in being unsure of your footing and then when you do slip, the reason you fell was because you were unsure of your footing. If you have ever seen people walk on an icy sidewalk, some people seem to manage quite well while others slip all over the place. It's not a question of what shoes they have on although sensible shoes are a good idea. It's a question of confidence. The man who is surefooted will not fall over. The man who is worried about the potential of falling will.

As an exercise in seeing things differently, I am going to make several statements below that are just hypothetical statements. What I want you to do is write down your response. Then I shall tell you a more ideal response that reinforces self-esteem. I think that one of the most confident people that I know taught me this trick and it will help you considerably to understand other people and to understand yourself. Read the situation and write down how you would react to it.

Someone criticizes the way that you dress, would you

a) Get flustered and be very embarrassed about it

b) Understand that different people have different tastes

c) Be polite, but feel really self-conscious

Someone says that you have done something wrong, even though you know that you haven't, would you:

a) Assume that they were right and do it again

b) Explain the way that you did it

c) Be polite and thank them for their input

You have been told at work that you have to do extra days. Do you:

a) Take the extra load with no complaint

b) Ask how you will be compensated for it

c) Agree but only if there can be some give and take in the situation

Your partner tells you that guests are coming tonight and the house is a mess. Do you:

a) Rush around and try to get the place cleaned up

b) Order food from a caterer so that you have less worry

c) Tell him that it's unreasonable at such short notice

In all of these examples, you are being put under stress and these are the kind of things where internalizing is unhealthy. The answers that you should choose are those which, with careful consideration, put you back in control of the situation, without leaving you with negativity to think over in your mind. Do not let things that happen within the course of your day make you negative. If there is a way out of a situation that suits everyone, try to find it. There are a few things that you need to know about reactions that will help you to stop creating negativity in your mind:

1) Do not assume the worst when something negative happens.

2) Do not assume responsibility when something negative happens until you know whose fault it really is.

3) Do not think about the negative aspect of what happened. Look for solutions. That way you are concentrating on something positive.

4) Do not retort in anger or frustration. You are likely to dig the hole even deeper.

5) Give yourself time to think about the situation. If you can't find an answer, try to meditate for a short while

and let your subconscious mind come up with an answer.

6) Do not react. If someone is feeding your negativity intentionally, giving them no instant reaction will prove less interesting to them.

The process by which you live your life should be from one moment to the next. If you waste a moment in regret or negative thinking, then that moment will soon be gone and you can never get it back again. Instead of doing this, think positively. If you are wrong, apologize and that's the end to the situation. If you haven't done anything wrong, don't let people walk over you.

When people develop self-esteem issues, they automatically assume blame when a lot of the time the only thing that they are to blame for is thinking so badly of themselves. You need more confidence and if you work your way through this book again, there are loads of tips and exercises that will help you to gain that confidence. When you do, you will begin to see life from a very different perspective.

Chapter 20 – Recommended reading

I have included this chapter because there is a very good book that can help you in your journey. The Writer's Way, by Julie Cameron, is a delight. Why would you need it if you have this book? Well, what it offers is something very special. If you have the version that has the journal, you are encouraged to write thoughts into the journal and get rid of negative thoughts in a very specific way. I don't want to take credit for something that is not original thinking but I do want to show you that there are ways to regain control of your life. The author introduces a system, which means that you organize a date with yourself every day and give yourself time to air your thoughts.

In fact one of the exercises that was suggested in the book is very useful and although it may sound a little random, what it does is teach you to get rid of thoughts that are getting in the way of your next positive experience. When you wake in the morning, either sit at the computer or write into a journal the first things that enter your head. These should not be thought out. Hold the pen above the paper and just let the words flow. Often we hold in a lot of negative thoughts and feelings and you may be surprised at the things that you will write, using your subconscious mind rather than actually planning them. Then, when you have read what you have written, screw it up or delete it because it's not the thoughts that matter and we don't want you to dwell on them as this isn't the point. The point is that it's a little like getting rid of the extra milk when a pan of milk is about to boil over. It allows you the freedom to start thinking afresh for the new day.

There are other books that you may find are very valuable as well. The Prophet by Kahlil Gibran is one of them. This is almost poetical and very philosophical, but don't let that put you off. When I first read this book, I did so on the suggestion of someone else and didn't know what to expect. I was expecting some kind of mumbo jumbo about religion or something like that but I was judging the book on the name rather than anything else. What I got was a complete surprise because the book goes through the kind of things that can happen to people within their day to day lives and has a lot of philosophical answers that are basically common sense, but written in such a poetic way that you feel pulled into that way of thinking and that's really healthy for people who are stressed or who have self-esteem issues. If you are not convinced, Google quotations by this man and you will no doubt be persuaded that the book may just hold answers for you that are important.

There are many inspirational works that can help you, but I really do recommend the books above – one because it gives you an inspiring place to write your journal and the other because it gives you inspirational thoughts.

Apart from these, go through the chapters of this book several times, because it's a lot of information to take in on the first reading. The thing that you need to remember to help you through stress and through self-esteem issues is that any negative thought from you is not helping your cause. You need to replace these with positive thoughts by turning your thoughts around to make them positive.

"I can't" becomes "I can try"

"I am incapable" becomes "I can do more when I learn more"

"I am not good enough" becomes "I am as good as I decide that I am"

At the end of the day, you have to accept responsibility. I have known people go through all of their lives harboring a chip on their shoulders about their past. This negativity bites away at the subconscious and fuels their inner turmoil. Instead of allowing negative things to do that to you, you really have to learn to let go. Own the problems that are yours to own and do something about them. As for the negativity placed on you by others, you need to let those people who feed you with negativity be the people who take ownership of that negativity. Don't let it enter your head for a moment that it's anything other than THEIR negativity.

We go through a very stressful lifestyle, though those who have stepped beyond the normal type of thinking that is dictated by the media and by society expectations of people actually find that there's not really a lot of truth in the standards that are set by society. There is no ruling that you should conform to a certain size and yet people diet for years because of their belief in this theory. There is no ruling that says that you should dress in a certain way, think in a certain way or act in a certain way and if you find that way isn't something that suits you, you need to implement your own rules, ones which are acceptable and which hurt no one.

If you do take up meditation or yoga, you will find that you are much calmer about your life and will let others dictate less what your values are. Yoga and meditation bring you closer to harmony within yourself and that's vital when you want to get beyond stress and self-esteem issues.

The books recommended in this section are secondary to finding yourself by looking very closely at what is making you negative and what is stressing you. You do need to study this before you try tackling the problems. For example, if you feel of less value, why do you feel it? Work out the roots of the problem. If your parents criticized you when you were a child, then you need to learn to move on. It was your parent's perception rather than a true perception of who you are. You have now grown up and have brought too much baggage with you through your life that you need to let go of.

The next time that someone says something negative to you, try another approach. Let it be their negativity rather than absorbing it and making it yours. It only harms your self-esteem levels when you allow it to. One of my relatives has gone through over fifty years carrying with her the negativity that she experienced during her youth. When her mother died, she found that this was the first time that she was able to let go. She was telling me about how liberating it felt, but as we talked, I could see that she had taken all the criticism of her childhood to heart over half a century and no matter what people told her, she never felt that she could live up to her parent's expectations.

When her mother was gone, however, she said that she realized the folly of keeping hold of her unhappiness because the person who disapproved of her so long ago was no longer around. She didn't have to live up to her mother's expectations. She also realized that she should have dropped the negativity years ago and not let it get in the way of her own happiness. Her advice to people in a situation such as hers is to drop the negativity now, because if you don't, you never live in the moment. Life passes all too quickly and you don't have time to take on the negativity that others impose upon you.

"Live life for now. Make sure that you know who you are and what you are capable of because at the end of the day, that's what matters. If you are happy to be the person that you are – don't let other people's lives impose upon yours. I did this for years and I effectively lost 50 years of my life that could have been rich with discovery. Instead, I chose to live in the shadow of a sister and let the criticism of my mother dictate the level of my happiness." Don't let your life become what other people see it to be. It isn't. Your life is something that you own and others should never have the power over you that take away your freedom from being who you are.

Conclusion

In this book, you have learned several ways to deal with fears, anxiety and self-consciousness or self-esteem issues. However, there is more to this and in this conclusion, I want to teach you about awareness and mindfulness. As you go through your life, be aware of your surroundings. Be aware of tastes, aromas and all of things that follow you into each moment of your life. By thinking about and being aware of each moment, rather than leaping into the past or worrying about the future, you begin to see all the positive things that surround you and make life very worthwhile. You define your life. It is not defined by other people's interpretations and as you go forward in your life, you find that space where you can actually breathe and enjoy the life that you have been gifted with.

You have probably heard the expression about "smelling the roses." People go through their lives letting stresses and strains take precedence over actually allowing their senses to enjoy what nature offers. It is important to do this because it helps you to negate the possibility of negative thoughts. If you are in a park, look at the flowers, enjoy the sounds of laughter of children. Notice the sun shining through the clouds. Be aware of shadows and of all of the elements of nature that surround you.

There is something to be said about listening to the world and absorbing the beauty of it all. All of the time that you close your doors on the world because of your self-esteem issues, you also deny yourself from the possibility that nature will help you to find the answers to all dilemmas as and when they may occur. You cut yourself off, you think negative thoughts and solutions seem impossible to find. Open the doors to possibility: enjoy the sunshine, the stars that hang in the sky at night and the stillness of darkness. Enjoy the sounds of the crickets and even the sound of your own breathing and you become so much more aware of what life is. It is astounding. It is an opportunity you only get once and nature helps you to gain confidence and in the stillness of thought, surrounded by beauty, your mind will find the answers to all of your dilemmas. You will learn to trust your inner instincts and that will take you a long way toward the stepping stones that lead forward.

It is a good idea to remind yourself to be aware. A note on the fridge that will greet you in the morning may help you. In an episode of Ally McBeal, she was asked by a psychiatrist to associate a happy song to bad moments. Although that may work short term, it is far better to be aware of the moment you are in and soak in everything that's around you because when you do that, you become more at harmony with life and with all your own senses, and this helps you to get away from negativity.

Practiced on a regular basis, you begin to learn that yesterday's mistakes can be left behind and that today is all you have. If you waste it on fear and self-esteem issues, it does not leave you much room for pleasure. Happier people are usually much more aware of their surroundings than people who are unhappy. As you become happier, you attract happiness. People like you because of your positive influence and you begin to lose that horrible feeling that you do not measure up. We all measure up. We are all perfect human beings. Even those who cannot walk or are born blind or crippled are equal and can enjoy the world that is offered to the same extent. In fact, those who have loss of senses often compensate with other senses and are more sensitive to life's pleasures than others. When you become a positive person, the folks who are attracted to you will also be positive people to reinforce your sense of worth and happiness and that is really all there is to dropping fears or letting them get in the way of living life to the fullest.

You may also have learned the expression "cup half full" as opposed to "cup half empty" and this is the way that people view their lives from an optimistic and a pessimistic point of view. Whenever you think something negative, you are taking the role of the pessimist. Try to turn it around and make whatever comes your way into something positive and what you are effectively doing is seeing the cup half full.

Here are some instances that may happen in your life where you can change the way that you look at your life and make it more positive:

Negative way of looking at things	Positive way of looking at things
I am too fat and need to lose weight	There is more of me to love
I am not very intelligent	I learn something new every day
I am not as good as my sister	My sister and I are different but both equally valuable as humans
My friends use me	I can be useful to friends who give equally

I don't like my life very much	I can get out and discover new things to improve my life
I am lonely	Being on my own gives me time to discover who I am
I am stressed	All things will pass. The unhappy periods of life are stepping stones to true happiness

I leave you with some quotations that may also give you food for thought on the subjects of self-esteem, confidence and happiness. May your journey toward finding your inner self be a productive one. You are the center of your own universe and these quotations may help you to see that.

"You can search throughout the entire universe for someone who is more deserving of your love and affection than you are yourself, and that person is not to be found anywhere. You, yourself, as much as anybody in the entire universe, deserve your love and affection." ~ Gautama Buddha

"There is no magic cure, no making it all go away forever. There are only small steps upward; an easier day, an unexpected laugh, a mirror that doesn't matter anymore." ~Laurie Halse Anderson

"Everything that happens to you is a reflection of what you believe about yourself. We cannot outperform our level of self-esteem. We cannot draw to ourselves more than we think we are worth." ~ Iyanla Vanzant

"As long as you look for someone else to validate who you are by seeking their approval, you are setting yourself up for disaster. You have to be whole and complete in yourself. No one can give you that. You have to know who you are - what others say is irrelevant." ~ Nic Sheff

Look at the above quotation because in the case of people having self-esteem issues, it is very relevant indeed. You are a wonderful human being even if you have not yet discovered that wonder. Don't expect people to validate who you are. If you look in a mirror you will only see what they see. Look deeper and see who you truly are for yourself without depending upon their validation. You are an individual. You are allowed to be different. In fact, if you think that you are different, it's an asset not a liability. Go forward in your life and when things stress you, close your eyes and see a time that gives you comfort. When you feel self-esteem issues, remember that people who are not kind to themselves will always be unhappy. Be kind to others, but most of all remember, you have to live with you for all the days of your life, so you need to be extra kind to yourself.

I hope that this book has brought you some kind of comfort and that you will do the exercises outlined in the book. They were written to help you to move forward. Consider this purchase as your starting line. From this moment onwards, you need to live your life to its fullest, never being afraid to be YOU. You are the cornerstone to your own life and cannot afford to allow its roots to become shallow, nor its foundations to become shaky because of what other people said. Smile as you move toward your new life from this moment on, and let yourself shine. You have the power within you to overcome stress and to live free of self-esteem issues once you take the reins of your life.

RECOMMENDED READING

Self Esteem: Self Confidence: Overcome Fear, Stress & Anxiety: Self Help Guide

hyperurl.co/self-esteem

HEALING: Heal Your Mind, Heal Your Body: Change Your Life

hyperurl.co/selfhealing

Boundaries: Line Between Right And Wrong
hyperurl.co/boundaries

PSYCHOPATH: Manipulation, Con Men And Relationship Fraud
smarturl.it/psychoa

You May Enjoy James Seal's Other Books

Personality Disorders: Borderline Personality Disorder: Beauty Queen or Emotional Terrorist?

hyperurl.co/emotionalterror

NLP Subconscious Mind Power: Change Your Mind Change Your Life

hyperurl.co/NLP

Creativity : Creative Thinking To Improve Memory, Increase Success and Live A Healthy Life

hyperurl.co/creative

Personality Disorders: NARCISSISM: How To Survive A Narcissistic Relationship

hyperurl.co/narcissism

Psychopath: Inside The Mind Of Predators and Con Men: Personality Disorders

hyperurl.co/psychopath

16144894R00089

Printed in Great Britain
by Amazon